CW00456546

# ANCIENT EGYPT

*Discover Fascinating History, Mythology, Gods, Goddesses, Pharaohs, Pyramids, and More from the Mysterious Ancient Egyptian Civilization*

**History Brought Alive**

# Free Bonus from HBA:
# Ebook Bundle

Greetings!

First of all, thank you for reading our books. As fellow passionate readers of history and mythology we aim to create the very best books for our readers.

Now, we invite you to join our VIP list. As a welcome gift we offer the History & Mythology Ebook Bundle below for free. Plus you can be the first to receive new books and exclusives! <u>Remember it's 100% free to join.</u>

Simply follow the link below to join.

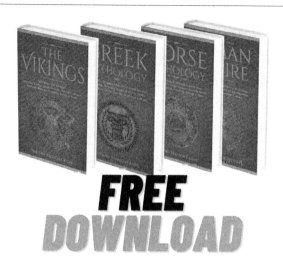

acknowledge that the author is not engaged in the rendering of legal, financial, medical or professional advice. The content within this book has been derived from various sources. Please consult a licensed professional before attempting any techniques outlined in this book.

By reading this document, the reader agrees that under no circumstances is the author responsible for any losses, direct or indirect, that are incurred as a result of the use of the information contained within this document, including, but not limited to, errors, omissions, or inaccuracies.

# Table of Contents

# Introduction

What does your bucket list look like? No matter your circumstances in life, it's there if you allow yourself even a moment to dream. Chances are, you're thinking about it right now! The bucket list is our repository of dreams. A to-do list not of things we feel we should do, like the New Year's resolutions we struggle to keep, but of the things we want to accomplish, given an opportunity, before we die. It speaks to the secret yearning of our hearts: A yearning to make or renew connections with others, to overcome our innermost fears, to escape the mundane day-to-day of our workday lives, or, just once, to experience the far-flung or the exotic. The stronger that heart's desire, the closer we place that dream to the top of our list. Your bucket list might include 20 things, or 100, or only one. No matter, it's yours. So let me ask again: what's on your bucket list? If you're like the thousands–affectionately labeled "Buckaroos"–who responded to that same question on bucketlist.net, you might have included some once-in-a-lifetime adventure like skydiving, zip-lining, scuba diving, or swimming with dolphins. Or perhaps your dream is more personal and long-term, such as getting married, buying a house, even getting a tattoo! But I'll wager that, like the vast majority of Buckaroos out there, somewhere near the top of your bucket list of longing is this: travel. And not just any kind of travel. Northern lights? The Grand Canyon? Nice. But that's not it. A cruise? You're not "feeling it." So let me tell you one thing (maybe the only thing) that I'm sure is on your list: you want to see the pyramids in Egypt. How do I know? No, I'm not psychic! I know because you picked up this book. And here's another thing of which I'm sure: You'll be glad you did!

Let me tell you why.

The pyramids rank among the largest, most majestic calling cards on earth. More than 13 million tourists from around the world flocked to the Nile Valley in 2019 to experience the tombs, temples, and treasures of Egypt, in particular the last remaining of the Seven Wonders of the Ancient World, the Pyramid of Khufu. Until the completion of the Cathedral Church of the

Blessed Virgin Mary of Lincoln (aka the Lincoln Cathedral) in northeastern England in 1311 CE (the Common Era), this aptly-named Great Pyramid of Giza held the distinction of being the tallest free-standing man-made structure on the planet. Its iconic profile dominated the earthscape for somewhere between 3851 and 3871 years! We'll get up close and personal with this and other pyramids in chapter 6. Suffice it to say that these glorious artifacts are the lodestone which draws us inexorably toward that mysterious, magnificent world of ancient Egypt with its gods and goddesses, kings and queens, temples and tombs, mythology and ritual, history, hieroglyphs and, running through it all, a river–the river–the source of all that was and is Egyptian civilization. In chapter 1, we'll journey together down this river through time and space to understand the meaning of Herodotus' words, "Egypt is the Nile, and the Nile is Egypt" (Gemmill, 1928, p. 295). Ancient Egypt, the second-oldest civilization on earth, endured and thrived for more than 3,000 years! You want to get closer to that fantastic, colorful, and mysterious time–to pull back the curtain and catch a glimpse of what it was really like back then. The problem is that you don't know where to begin. You're overwhelmed! You want more than a superficial, watered-down Wikipedia rehash. Yet, you haven't the time or energy to dig through a mountain of scholarly tomes written by Egyptologists, or to navigate some tortuous maze of footnotes. You're searching for that one book, the starting place of that bucket list dream to experience the ancient Egyptian civilization which produced the pyramids and so much more.

This is that one book. Within these pages are the kind of vibrant, exciting, and memorable characters, places, and events that put flesh on what might otherwise be the dry bones of ancient Egyptian history. That's because we at History Brought Alive share a passion for presenting rigorously factual, meticulously researched, and thoroughly enjoyable history and culture in an easy-to-digest style that keeps you turning the page until the very end. It's what sets us apart from the competition!

What sets this book, in particular, apart from others is its unique approach to unfolding the successive eras of Egyptian history. The traditional editorial strategy has been to distill that history into conventional and sometimes monotonous timelines, chronologies, alphabetized glossaries, and so on. Granted, navigating the lives and reigns (sometimes concurrent or, at least, overlapping) of almost 200 pharaohs requires that historians impose some sort of structure on the facts! The first to grapple with that monumental task was a 3rd century BCE (Before the Common Era) Egyptian priest named Manetho, who grouped the pharaonic succession before Alexander the Great into 30 dynasties. To his credit, that convention has endured to the present day. Modern historians have further organized these dynasties into periods so that, for example, the reigns of the eight kings of the First Dynasty (2950-2750) and the eight or more of the Second Dynasty (2750-2650) become part of the Early Dynastic Period. So the question is: Are you bored yet or, worse, having flashbacks to your tenth grade history class? We hear you. These scholarly conventions are extremely useful, but they don't fully deliver on our History Brought Alive promise to make your journey through ancient Egypt exciting and memorable. Allow us, then, to take a slightly different approach: a dramatic approach. Yes, there will be names and dates too. But we promise that when you've finished reading this book, you'll not take away a kitbag of dusty facts–you'll own the experience as if you've lived it yourself! So then, think about this: The timeline of ancient Egyptian history is precisely like the script of an epic theatrical production when you examine it from a bird's-eye view.

Egyptian history as high drama? Nothing could be closer to the truth! In the coming chapters, you'll become familiar with the broad outlines and the key players in that drama played out over millennia on what might just be the world's grandest outdoor stage. But it requires the proper perspective to appreciate it. So here's an analogy drawn from the very geography of Egypt: Though ancient Egyptians had never seen their country from above, they imagined the course of the Nile River, from where they believed it originated in the underground caverns of Hapy, god of the inundation, near the First Cataract, to the lazy, slow-moving Delta where it drained into the Mediterranean Sea, to resemble a papyrus stalk in full flower; and its most northerly tributary, which ends in the Faiyum Lake, a new shoot growing from that stalk (Wilkinson, Toby, 2015). It was only when I saw a satellite image of that same country, as the camera panned slowly southward from lower to upper Egypt (remember, the Nile flows from south to north), that I could see, from miles above, the papyrus-flower, the new shoot, the slightly crooked stalk, precisely as those ancient Egyptians had pictured their homeland with their feet in the sand. Now I'll remember that perspective of Egypt for as long as I live. I own it. We'll be able to say the same of the broad sweep of the history of Egypt when we approach it from a similar vantage point.

I've drawn upon the chronology set forth by Professors Bob Brier and A. Hoyt Hobbs, which breaks Egyptian political history into nine eras (Brier & A Hoyt Hobbs, 2013) with their approximate periods and dynasties. I say approximate because, before the year 624 BCE, dates can fluctuate by 50-100 years, and many can only be inferred by comparing religious texts, inscriptions from the tombs of specific rulers, even the hieroglyphs on the walls of palace and temple ruins scattered throughout upper and lower Egypt. This inference creates some discrepancies between the chronologies of different historians. Nonetheless, the vast majority of experts are in agreement with the broader brushstrokes of the following Egyptian chronology, to which I've added a theatrical twist:

## Prologue

The Predynastic Era (before 3150 BCE) - Prehistory to Dynasty 0

Act I

The Early Dynastic Era (3150-2686 BCE) - Dynasties I-II

The Old Kingdom Era (2686-2181 BCE) - Dynasties III-VI

## First Intermission

The First Intermediate Period (2181-2040 BCE) - Dynasties VIII-XI

Act II

The Middle Kingdom Era (2040-1782 BCE) - Dynasties XI-XII

## Second Intermission

The Second Intermediate Period (1782-1570 BCE) - Dynasties XIII-XVII

Act III

The New Kingdom Era (1570-1070 BCE) - Dynasties XVIII-XX

**Epilogue**

The Late Period (1070-332 BCE) - Dynasties XXI-XXXI

The Ptolemaic Period (332-30 BCE) - Dynasties XXXII-XXXIII

The Late and Ptolemaic Periods taken together represent an era of gradual decline in Egyptian history, when foreign powers (Libya, Nubia, Persia, Greece, and, finally, Rome) began to assert direct influence, if not control, over pharaonic governance and the reshaping of cultural and religious norms. For this reason, some historians omit them altogether from chronologies which focus on indigenous ancient Egyptian political history. Instead, we have taken a broader view. While we will not detail this later period of Egyptian history, we consider it an appropriate epilogue to the classic Egyptian story. First, then, we'll look briefly at the famous last Pharaoh before the demise of ancient Egypt. Ultimately, with the death of Julius Caesar's widow, Cleopatra VII, in 30 BCE, and the murder of her son and co-regent Ptolemy Philopator Philometor Caesar ("Caesarion"), the last king of Egypt, that same year, the paradigm of pharaonic rule ends: The country becomes a mere province of the Roman Empire under Augustus, and the curtain falls forever on this 3100-year historical drama we have come to know as ancient Egypt.

We'll follow the intrigues of Caesar and Cleopatra, Mark Antony, Caesarion, and his great-uncle Octavian (later to become Emperor Augustus) through to the last scene at the end of chapter 6. But we mustn't get ahead of ourselves. Before Caesarion and Cleopatra; before the foreign rulers of ancient Egypt; before the Pharaohs; before Osiris, Isis, Horus and the host of Egyptian deities (chapter 3); before Amun, the "self-created," sitting cross-legged on the ben-ben which had risen from primordial waters, or any of the myriad myths which shaped the worldview of that civilization (chapter 4); before even the first representative of the genus *Homo* had stood on the rocky outcropping above the First Cataract and gazed down upon the future Land of the Pharaohs (chapter 2), there was a river.

As successive species of man moved through that river valley over hundreds of thousands of years—first, *erectus,* then *heidelbergensis, neanderthalensis,* and lastly, *sapiens*—they came to identify it as *the* River: *Iteru,* in the ancient Egyptian language of the modern humans who hunted and gathered on its floodplains and who later herded domesticated livestock and planted crops in its fertile alluvial soil. It was not until the Greeks under Alexander the Great conquered Egypt in 332 BCE and inaugurated the 300-year dynasty of the Ptolemies that their language gave *Neilos,* "the river," the name we recognize today: the Nile. Whether *Neilos, Iteru,* or another name given before the dawn of Egyptian history, this is the grand and glorious stage upon which we witness the birth, flourishing, and decline of earth's second-oldest civilization.

# Chapter 1: Setting the Stage

## Many Rivers, One River

"Without the Nile, there would be no Egypt" (Wilkinson, Toby, 2015, p. 3). That statement would seem bold were it not absolutely true. The river, *iteru* in the ancient Egyptian language, has dominated and defined the East African landscape since before the arrival of the first human species, *Homo erectus*, in Africa more than 700,000 years ago. The Egyptian segment of the Nile River follows a roughly straight, south-to-north course from modern Aswan to Cairo and the Delta. Seen from above, the river's course resembles the iconic papyrus reed with its slender stalk and flowering head–and, like that iconic water plant, was integral to ancient Egyptian civilization and thought. So true was this that the glyph for Egypt was simply a horizontal line (representing the flat floodplain) with three black circles beneath (signifying clumps of the black alluvial soil left behind after the annual inundation).

The waters of the river, and particularly of the annual inundation, were the lifeblood of Egypt. According to Harvey Cox, "the annual flooding of the Nile...provided the framework by which the society was held together" (Harvey Gallagher Cox, 2013, p. 27). Yet, ironically, no Egyptian in the nation's 3,000-year history ever knew the actual geographical source of the Nile, recognized today as the world's longest river at 4,130 miles (Liu et al., 2009). Nor would the average Egyptian citizen have acknowledged the need to know. Instead, an all-pervasive polytheism, which ascribed divine agency to every aspect of human experience, including the life-sustaining flow of the river, framed their worldview. "Sun gods, river goddesses, and astral deities abounded. History was subsumed under cosmology, society under nature, time under space. Both god and man were part of nature" (Harvey Gallagher Cox, 2013, p. 27).

That worldview convinced Egyptians that the river's life-giving (or sometimes life-taking) waters flowed from an underground cavern beneath the First Cataract, adjacent to the Elephantine island, close to Egypt's southern border with Nubia (modern Sudan). This underground cavern was the abode of the god Hapy—not the god of the Nile itself, but the annual inundation. Though no one had ever seen Hapy, pictograms depict this deity as a big-bellied, droopy-breasted figure of nonspecific gender who wore a ceremonial beard (Wilkinson, 2003). This depiction speaks to the Egyptian belief that Hapy (like the waters of *iteru* itself) was the source of fertility and prosperity. Nothing is more expressive of their conviction than the following excerpt from the "Hymn to Hapy (the Nile Flood)," originally written in Middle Egyptian and believed to have been composed during the Middle Kingdom period (c. 2060-1782 BCE):

*Hymn to Hapy*: Hail flood! emerging from the earth, arriving to bring Egypt to life, hidden of form, the darkness in the day, the one whose followers sing to him, as he waters the plants, created by Ra to make every herd live, who satisfies the desert hills removed from the water, for it is his dew that descends from the sky—he, the beloved of Geb, controller of Nepri, the one who makes the crafts of Ptah verdant....

If he is greedy, the whole land suffers, great and small fall moaning. People are changed at his coming; the one who creates him is Khnum. When he rises, then the land is in joy, then every belly is glad, every jaw has held laughter, every tooth revealed.

Of course, we need only consult a map to understand the reality which was literally beyond their comprehension: the one *iteru,* or river, of Egypt, the only Nile they knew, was the product of several major and minor tributaries which commingled far south in regions once occupied by ancient Nubia, the semi-mythical Land of Punt, and beyond the 'end of the world' as the Egyptian people knew it. The main branch of the Nile, called White for its heavy clay deposits, begins in a stream, the *Ruvyironza*, which flows out of Mount Kikizi in southern Burundi (Godfrey Mugoti, 2009) and empties into Lake Victoria. From Jinja, Lake Victoria, it flows into Lake Albert and then continues its northward journey until it joins the Blue Nile at Khartoum in Sudan–a distance of some 2,300 miles from its source. The Blue Nile, on the other hand, originates at Lake Tana in the highlands of modern-day Ethiopia and flows some 900 miles through Ethiopia and Sudan. It has historically provided at least 80 percent of the fresh water and silt in the Nile during the North African monsoon season between June and October. A third major Nile tributary, the Atbara River, called the Red Nile, starts its journey 500 miles southeast of the White Nile, in the mountains 30 miles north of Lake Tana in Ethiopia, as little more than a stream. However, like the Blue Nile to the south, it swells dramatically during the late summer rains, contributing to the surge of the annual inundation in the Nile Valley. The Yellow Nile, a former tributary that flowed from eastern Chad to its confluence at the southern point of the Great Bend of the White Nile between c. 8000 BCE and c. 1000 BCE (Keding, 2000), became extinct at roughly the same time as ancient Egyptian civilization was subsumed into the Roman Empire.

So there were many rivers, with many sources, each bearing her gifts–fresh, clear water, clay, black silt–in a happy marriage of currents, rushing through steep gorges and past red sandstone cliffs and, finally, tumbling around the crags of the First Cataract in Upper Egypt and on toward the Great Green, as Egyptians used to call the Mediterranean Sea. I think the ancient Egyptians would have smiled with pleasure had they been aware that the several tributaries of the White Nile (Blue, White, Red, and Yellow, among others), seen from above, resemble the roots of their beloved and iconic papyrus plant!

## Inundation

We'll return to the importance of the annual inundation throughout this book, as fundamental as it was to ancient Egypt's economic, social, political, and even religious development. But, if you're like me, you can't help but ask the question: *What was it like?* Reach out with your imagination to that distant time. Can you get a sense of the mystery–and for every Egyptian, it was indeed that–of the inundation? Consider the words of New Zealand filmmaker John Feeney:

Flowing out of a barren desert, from a source "beyond all known horizons," the Nile had baffled the world for thousands of years. Regular as sun and moon, in the middle of burning summer, without a drop of rain in sight, when all other rivers on earth were drying up, for no apparent reason at all, the Nile rose out of its bed every year, and for three months embraced all of Egypt (Feeney, 2006, par. 1).

Feeney and his Egyptian crew set out in 1964 to capture on film the last Nile flood and the last Egyptian inundation before the completion of the Aswan High Dam. He and his crew are the only persons in history to have followed the flood from its source in the Ethiopian highlands, all the way to Cairo, and to have documented the journey. His words are a stirring, if bitter-sweet, *in memoriam* to the singular event which shaped and defined a civilization:

With a name that means "roaring fire," the Tisisat Falls must be one of the loneliest places on Earth, little known and rarely seen by outsiders....We first heard the murmur and then the roar as we got our first glimpse through the trees.

Then we stood transfixed before the answer to the riddle that had baffled the world for thousands of years. There before us, pouring forth with the sound of thunder in one colossal fuming torrent, the Blue Nile was anything but blue, plunging from its source in Lake Tana above, down into a deep dark abyss that was the beginning of its great journey to Egypt (Feeney, 2006, par. 16-17).

He goes on to say that,

By August, the most colossal Nile flood of the century was pouring out of Ethiopia. We followed the surge as it moved like a slow-motion tidal wave across the deserts of eastern and northern Sudan into Egypt (Feeney, 2006, par. 19).

With the arrival of the inundation, dry land became lakes; basins filled and overflowed, filling adjacent basins. Villages, built on high ground, became islands (reminiscent of the Primordial Mound of creation, surrounded by turbulent, chaotic water), and neighbors visited one another in boats. The sounds of singing and celebration echoed throughout the Nile Valley. At last, when the waters had receded,

In the soft sediment left by the floodwaters...the farmers of Egypt...set about planting their crops of beans, wheat, and barley as they had done for thousands of years (Feeney, 2006, par. 24).

Theirs was an organic relationship with *iteru*, the river which carried life and happiness to the Egyptian people through waters that were not the country's own but came as gifts from afar.

## The Red Land

While the narrow strip of fertile land known as *Kemet*, "black land," was said to be the gift of the Nile, the surrounding desert, *Deshret*, "red land," would have been considered the opposite. Egyptians recognized that the western and eastern deserts presented a formidable (though not impenetrable) natural barrier to intruders, creating significant cultural isolation in which the unique Egyptian civilization could develop. Nonetheless, they viewed the red land as largely inhospitable. After all, they were the People of the Black Soil, and the fertility of the Nile Valley was the blessing of Hapy. The desert was dry, hot, and dangerous. It was also the abode of foreigners–Libyans to the west, nomadic tribes, and expanding empires like those of Babylonia, Assyria, and Persia to the north and east–who posed a threat, both real and perceived, to the security of ancient Egypt. That the Egyptians were willing to cross the unfamiliar and treacherous desert to exploit its natural resources, particularly gold, turquoise, lapis lazuli, and other precious materials, indicates how strong the attraction was to the elite of ancient Egypt. However, aside from its distant, buried treasures, the two obvious features of the Red Land that found meaning within the Egyptian worldview, and therefore ensured its enduring significance, were its aridity and location.

The Red Land was a desert adjacent to the western bank of the Nile and yet beyond the reach of the yearly inundation. As we'll see in chapter 8, this made it the ideal place for Egyptian burials. Remember our previous examination of the sand-pit graves of the Predynastic Period and before? Modern humans, who lived for millennia not only in the Nile Valley but in the broader surrounding desert lands, buried their dead in shallow pits dug into the sand, which served to desiccate, preserve, and, to some extent, naturally mummify the remains. Even when the *mastaba*, a sloped, four-sided stone structure resembling a bench, became a prevalent funerary structure, the body within was still buried in that same sand-pit, often covered with wooden planks which were themselves buried under a layer of sand. It was only later in the Old Kingdom as beliefs in the nature of the Afterlife evolved that the elite members of society–Pharaoh, his family, and wealthy citizens–began to construct tombs for above-ground burial.

Egyptian cemeteries were therefore deliberately established to the west of the Nile, on the fringes of the western desert. But the preservative effects of the desert sand were not the whole story of Egyptian burial practices. The Osiris-Isis mythology evolved into a paradigm of the preparation of the deceased for a conscious, physical existence in the Afterlife. First, the Pharaoh and, later, the Egyptian people as a whole, came to identify their death/rebirth experience with that of Osiris, Lord of the Underworld. He was called the Lord of the Westerners, the temporarily disembodied spirits of the deceased who waited in "the West" for an imminent rebirth into their previously preserved or mummified bodies. Egyptian burial customs reiterated and reinforced the belief that resurrection would come from the west, the Red Land direction. Bodies of deceased individuals were transported by boat from the west to the east bank of the Nile, where they were placed in the hands of embalmers. Then, following an intricate preparation process, tailored to the family's financial resources, the mummified body was transferred once again to a boat and carried across the Nile, toward the west, where the family enacted a ritual drama before the interment of the remains. It is ironic that, while the life of every Egyptian came from the Black Land, *Kemet*, the new life which all eagerly sought for and anticipated was believed to come from *Deshret*, the Red Land.

# Chapter 2: Egypt at the Dawn of History

## What Came Before

Artifacts uncovered in and near the narrow floodplain which hugs the eastern and western banks of the Nile, from the rocky, turbulent First Cataract in the south to the broad, fan-shaped delta in the north attest to an early human presence in, and dependence upon, the land. The unique geography of the world's longest river (Liu et al., 2009) facilitated the dispersion of *Homo erectus* ("upright-walking man"), as early as 700,000 years ago, through eastern Africa into the Levant (modern-day Israel, Palestine, Lebanon, Syria and much of southeastern Turkey), India, and eventually to

Java, where the most recent *H. erectus* fossils have been found. Unfortunately, no such fossilized remains have yet been uncovered in the region, which later would be known as Egypt. However, the discovery throughout the Nile Valley of distinctively pear-shaped, flaked, flint hand-axes believed to be associated with *H. erectus* suggests that these early nomadic hunter-gatherers passed through the valley over thousands of years. At that time, the terrain surrounding the river more closely resembled savannah than the arid, desertified climate we know today, and large populations of gazelle, hartebeest, giant buffalo (*pelorovis),* and other grazing mammals provided ample food supply.

*Homo heidelbergensis*, which exhibited some features of *H. erectus* but which possessed a larger braincase, coexisted with its possible ancestor for at least a half-million years, until around 200,000 BCE, and must have transited the Nile Valley since evidence of its presence in the Levant dates back to 790, 000 BCE (Smithsonian's National Museum of Natural History, 2010). *H. heidelbergensis* may have been more communal than its predecessor, building hearths and demonstrating the earliest human control of fire. They were likewise more innovative: more significant refinements to the flint hand-ax, and the manufacture of wooden spears, speaks to the evolution of early human skill with hunting. Thus, *H. heidelbergensis* has the distinction of being the first big game hunter.

Around 400,000 BCE, while *H. heidelbergensis* endured colder nights and frigid winter temperatures in Europe and the northern Mediterranean area, subtle evolutionary genetic processes were at work. One outcome of these processes was another branch of the *Homo* family tree: a robust and resourceful species called *H. neanderthalensis,* or Neanderthals as we have come to know them. Neanderthals were distributed through Europe (their name comes from the Neander Valley in Germany, where their remains were first identified) and in parts of southwest and central Asia (Smithsonian's National Museum of Natural History, 2010), where the discovery of their more sophisticated stone tool technology, called Mousterian as opposed to the archaic Acheulean hand-ax technology of *H. erectus*, attests to their presence there (*Mousterian Pluvial*, 2021). Neanderthals exhibited a somewhat more refined, but not radically different, way of life than their ancestors. They lived in a community, built shelters, controlled fire, and hunted big game using spears. Forensic examination of Neanderthal skeletal development shows that they used these spears by thrusting, not by throwing, from which we can infer two things: Neanderthals must have routinely gotten up close and personal with their prey, and they must have hunted collaboratively, that is, in larger groups, to succeed.

Neanderthal tool technology–particularly scrapers, used to remove animal flesh from hides–uncovered in the Western Sahara, close to the Nile Valley, points to Neanderthals' presence from around 70,000 BCE until 43,000 BCE. Unfortunately, the conspicuous absence of Neanderthals from the Nile Valley region after that time coincides with the arrival of the first modern humans (Brier, 1999), the outworking of whose earlier Cognitive Revolution (Harari, 2014) equipped them to out-compete their genetic cousins, driving them to extinction. There is no evidence of *H. neanderthalensis* in the fossil record, anywhere in the world, after about 30, 000 BCE.

Where did these new kids on the block come from? The Omo Valley of southern Ethiopia evidences what has proven to be the watershed moment in the history of the world, close to 200,000 years ago, with the first appearance of *Homo sapiens*, called 'Anatomically-Modern Humans', to differentiate them from later, post-cognitive-revolution *Homo sapiens sapiens,* called modern humans, who appeared between 70,000 BCE and 30,000 BCE in Eastern Africa. The former shared many of the cultural characteristics of their *H. heidelbergensis* ancestors, yet seemed to make hardly a ripple, as it were, on the genetic pond until the Cognitive Revolution (Harari, 2014). "But then," says Harari, "beginning about 70,000 years ago, *Homo sapiens* started doing very special things." (Harari, 2014, p. 19). Concerning those who remained in Eastern Africa after the departure of *H. sapiens* bands during the second "Out-of-Africa" event around 65,000 BCE (University of Cologne, 2021), and who migrated into the Nile Valley around 43,000 BCE, archaeological evidence bears witness to dramatic advances in tool technology and manufacture, hunting practices, crafting of pottery, the grinding of pigments for cosmetic and ceremonial uses, and burial of the dead (I. Shaw, 2000).

At approximately the time of the Out-of-Africa migration, around 65,000 BCE, the Western Sahara was lush with vegetation thanks to cyclical climatic and environmental processes, which turned the once-arid landscape into green savannah. When *H. sapiens* first arrived in the Nile region, that cycle had reversed itself, bringing the return of arid and less habitable conditions beyond the fringes of the valley. Climatic changes reduced the Nile river flow throughout this time, but evidence supports that men used fishing to provide food for their families. The people lived together in smaller bands of 25-50 persons. They were still hunters and gatherers, but their larger brains and cognitive hard-wiring enabled them to innovate in terms of how those subsistence methods were carried out and the technology they used. For example, men had moved away from cutting chert blanks, which would later be fashioned into rudimentary axes and blades, favoring more durable and sharper materials such as obsidian, flint, or quartzite. During this time, men had discovered how to make a sickle, presumably to harvest wild grains. The agricultural revolution was thousands of years in the future!

However, the most extraordinary development thus far had come about simultaneously with the Cognitive Revolution: the bow and arrow. Archaeologists place the invention of the bow and arrow at somewhere around 70,000 BC–coincidentally, about the same time as development of our species. It represented a significant step forward in hunting technology. Do you remember that we discussed previously how Neanderthals, for instance, developed an exaggerated skeletal structure on one side of their bodies? It came from repeated thrusting of their spears to capture and kill their prey. Neanderthals, it seems, could not grasp the concept of a projectile, something that left your hand on its way to taking down your dinner. After all, they were concrete thinkers; they literally could not imagine such a sophisticated hunting tool as a bow. Neanderthal physiology would suggest that they hadn't figured out the idea of throwing their spear instead of thrusting. *H. sapiens* figured everything out. Arrow points no larger than a thumbnail ("micro-points") have been discovered at Kom Ombo on the south-central Nile, which attests to *H. sapiens'* advanced skills.

Hunter-gatherers lived in and around the Nile Valley over the next 30,000-35,000 years, through cycles of aridity and greening of the deserts and fluctuations in the Nile river flow. Identification of their cultural developments centered on the particular regions or ancient cities where archaeologists found their artifacts, mainly pottery. However, the names of their bands or tribes are lost to time. The Nile Valley seems to have been uninhabited for 2,000 years or more, between approximately 11,000 BCE and 9,000 BCE when the river experienced extreme flooding. As a result, people were forced into the Western Desert, which was still more habitable during this period. When the waters receded, people moved back into the lower valley and settled around the lake formed by a natural basin known as the Faiyum depression. Their culture is known as Faiyum A (c. 9000-6000 BCE). Domestic cattle, sheep, and goats were introduced into Egypt late in this period, where the people had before subsisted by hunting, gathering, and fishing. They built reed huts with underground grain storage cellars and crafted distinctive pottery. Bans of nomadic hunter-gatherers settled around Faiyum lake, forming communities with centralized government by tribal chieftains.

The Faiyum period in Lower Egypt gave way to the Merimda (c. 5,000 BCE-4,000 BCE) and, later, the El-Omari, Ma'adi, and Tasian cultures (c. 4,000 BCE). More durable pole-framed huts with windbreaks, organized into rows, replaced the reed huts of the Faiyum period. Later still, villagers used walls of plastered mud to construct oval huts with woven floor and wall coverings. The ceramic design continued to flourish. People developed more extensive and more secure grain storage facilities. Around this time, cemeteries were more widely used to bury the dead.

When the Merimda culture was at its midpoint in Lower Egypt, the Badarian culture (c. 4,500 BCE - 4,000 BCE) flourished further south, becoming Upper Egypt. These were farmers, supplementing their primary grain diets with hunting. Perhaps their location closer to the Nile headwaters favored a more substantial flow of water to reach further inland and a significantly higher proportion of alluvium. They lived in tents after the fashion of their nomadic ancestors. Domesticated animals provided food and materials for shelters. Like their northern contemporaries, the Badarian people buried their dead in cemeteries, atop mats of reeds, or covered with animal hides. Unlike them, however, the people of Badarian culture included food offerings and personal belongings, presaging the burial practices of the Early Kingdom period.

The following 850 years saw the rapid development of predynastic culture in Upper Egypt through the Naqada I (c. 4,000 BCE - 3,500 BCE), Naqada II (c. 3,500 BCE - 3,200 BCE), and Naqada III (3,200 BCE - 3,150 BCE) periods. More sophisticated dwellings with hearths and possibly windows progressed to sun-baked, mud-brick homes. Mummification began around 3,500 BCE, and graves were becoming more ornate. Abydos, north of Naqada, became a significant and vital burial center for people all over the country. Future power centers were developing at Thinis, Naqada, and Nekhen, and people wrote a prototypical hieroglyphic language at Abydos. As these smaller communities grew into "nomes," tribal centers under the authority of "nomarchs" or chieftains, war broke out between the nomes at Thinis, Naqada, and Nekhen. The nomarch of Thinis believed to have been Menes/Narmer, and his tribe defeated that of Naqada and subsequently assimilated Nekhen. The Scorpion Kings I and II waged war against Menes/Narmer and an individual named Ka. Narmer defeated these predynastic kings to establish a politically unified Upper and Lower Egypt, ruled from Thinis where he had previously been nomarch, inaugurating the First Dynasty of ancient Egypt. Archaeology supports this sequence of events: A study of pottery fragments from digs in Lower Egypt reveals a dramatic and complete transformation in manufacturing style around Narmer's victory, from the localized Tasian culture to that of Upper Egyptian Naqada III (I. Shaw, 2000).

# The People of the Black Soil

## Social Structure

We must not impose our western concepts of social structure upon ancient Egyptian society.

There was no recognizable class system, with its upper, middle and lower strata, though, even in the Predynastic Period, we see evidence in Egyptian burials of a developing hierarchical structure based on wealth. Instead, the fabric of Egyptian society was woven upon a framework of rights and freedoms, the nature and extent of which defined the social category to which an individual man or woman belonged. The real possibility of upward (or, at times, downward) movement between categories is a distinguishing feature of ancient Egyptian civilization, in stark contrast to the modern-day caste system of some eastern cultures, which is rigid and inflexible. Of the four categories of ancient Egyptian social structure, defined by the relative possession of these rights and freedoms, the ones that offer the slightest chance of mobility are slaves and royalty.

**Royalty**

Royalty was the narrowest social category, encompassing the immediate family of the reigning Pharaoh, his parents, and full aunts and uncles. The chief of Pharaoh's many wives was considered royalty as well; his other wives were not. A commoner who married to become Pharaoh's chief wife was granted royalty, as was the common wife of an individual who assumed the throne after their marriage. The royal family was given full economic support while they lived together in palatial accommodations, yet they retained the right to work if they chose. The granting of power to royal family members was not automatic; many had to work to demonstrate proficiency and earn promotions. Work most often involved government positions, from which the family member or Pharaoh himself could exercise leverage over government departments. This was especially true of Pharaoh's sons, all of whom would be groomed so that one or another–usually, but not always, the eldest– could succeed his father in the pharaonic dynasty, either reigning concurrently with or upon the death of his father.

**Free Citizens**

Two things defined free Egyptian citizens: the right to travel and the right to enter into contractual arrangements such as buying or selling property or other possessions, buildings, or animals. Free citizens, therefore, exercised some control over their own lives, unlike serfs and slaves. They could also enter into marriage contracts with the parents of a prospective spouse. In this regard, men and women enjoyed equal rights under the law while, on the other hand, occupations were strictly gender-defined: women performed all the duties of managing their households, while men engaged in outside occupations such as farming, herding, craftsmanship, or business. It is estimated that slightly under half of the Egyptian population consisted of free citizens by the Middle and New Kingdom Periods.

## Serfs

Serfs did not control their lives but were completely controlled; they had no freedom to initiate legal, contractual arrangements, including marriage, though they could choose to live with a partner and raise children. However, a free citizen could decide to marry a serf, whom the master must first free. According to Brier, "serfs belonged to the land, hence changed masters only as the land changed hands" (Brier & A Hoyt Hobbs, 2013). Masters expected absolute obedience from their serfs, who were considered their property. Nevertheless, serfs could, and did, attain the status of free citizens through the good graces of their masters who might elevate them to positions of responsibility and authority. Or a serf might distinguish himself on the battlefield, meaning his freedom in that way.

## Slaves

Slaves, like serfs, were under absolute control and could be bought, sold, and traded like chattel. They had no rights and no freedoms. Slavery, like serfdom, was a hereditary status; the children of slaves were automatically slaves themselves. Because only foreigners captured in war could be slaves, there were no slaves in the Early Kingdom days of Egypt since she had not yet flexed her military muscle against other peoples and taken captives. However, once Egypt had undertaken numerous military campaigns, the ranks of slaves grew and could be utilized in hard or dangerous labor situations, particularly mining or quarry work.

## At Least it's Work: Occupations in Egyptian Society

### Farmers

If Egypt is the gift of the Nile, then it is equally valid that farmers who cultivated the soil and grew their crops according to the clockwork regularity of the inundation were the gift of Egypt. Egyptians constructed their calendar entirely around the natural rhythms of the inundation and, therefore, of agriculture. Egypt had only three seasons, each consisting of four 30-day months. The first season of the year was called Akhet, the time of the inundation (Haney, n.d.). The first day of the new year corresponded to the arrival of the floodwaters at the First Cataract adjacent to Elephantine Island, in the far south of the country. Government clerks would watch for the water to surge around the rocks out of supposed underground caverns in which, according to Egyptian belief, the God of inundation, Hapy, lived to favor the people with this annual gift. From the first day that the waters began to rise–Egypt's New Year's Day–officials would periodically measure the height of the surge on a "Nilometer" that measured in cubits the magnitude of the inundation. Such officials communicated the information gathered to Pharaoh and his government officials, who devised estimates of the coming year's agricultural productivity. These estimates, in turn, formed the basis for the taxation of the people of Egypt at harvest.

Egyptians used two different types of Nilometer in ancient Egypt, depending on the location along the river. The first was portable and could be repositioned to zero every year to account for increased water height due to the previous flooding sedimentary deposits. The second type of Nilometer was fixed rather than portable: It resembled a narrow stone staircase whose risers were carved with numbers to measure the height of the Nile in cubits. The lowermost stair indicated the zero point–the average level of the Nile before inundation. Unfortunately, less than thirty fixed Nilometers have been found intact from one end to the other of the Nile Valley.

Based on accumulated information from previous years, officials could estimate the success or disaster of that year's crops. If the water was too high, Egyptian people could anticipate extreme flooding, possibly losing life and income. If the Nile surge was lower than usual, it could mean ensuing famine. Reflecting upon the Nile's variability, Wilkinson quotes the Roman historian, Pliny, who observed that.

An average rise is one of sixteen cubits [twenty-seven feet]. A smaller volume of water does not irrigate all localities, and a larger one by retiring too slowly retards agriculture...in a rise of twelve cubits [Egypt] senses famine, and even at one of thirteen it begins to feel hungry, but fourteen cubits brings cheerfulness, fifteen complete confidence and sixteen delight. (Wilkinson, Toby, 2015)

As the inundation swept through the Nile Valley, making farming impossible, farmers would use the opportunity to repair their homes and tools and prepare for the next season, named *Peret,* or emergence (Haney, n.d.). Egypt had developed a system of irrigation canals to take the precious alluvial soils of the inundation further inland to cultivate a larger area of crops. Unfortunately, the sometimes-torrential waters of the inundation might have disturbed or damaged the canals or filled them with silt. Therefore, the first step of emergence was to dig out, repair, and reconstruct all their irrigation canals. When the water had finally receded, leaving behind the rich black soil that gave Egypt the name *Kemet* (Haney, n.d.), farmers would return to their fields to plow, then to break up the clods of moist earth, and finally to scatter seed into the furrows. If a farmer were fortunate to own cattle, they would do the work of pulling the plow while he leaned his weight on the back to ensure deep furrows. Usually, a son walked before the team, guiding it in straight lines. If a farmer had no cattle, two men would take their place in the traces to do the hard work of pulling. Once the women had scattered seeds into the furrows, they tossed straw over the top, encouraging their sheep to mash the seeds into the soft soil with their hooves. A period of waiting and anticipation followed planting, while farmers performed the strenuous daily task of nurturing their crops to harvest. Water needed to be drawn from the Nile in buckets and emptied into the canals. There were regular chores to occupy them while they waited for their crops to ripen– and, of course, there were always weeds to pull!

Finally, everyone welcomed the third and final season of the year, Shemu, the harvest (Haney, n.d.). Government officials would pass through the Nile Valley, measuring the fields and taxing them at the rate established months before on the first day of inundation. Once the officials' assessment was complete, entire families would move into the fields to harvest their crops before weather conditions or animals could affect them. Egyptian farmers utilized the same harvesting process 5000 years ago as is currently employed in many parts of Africa and the Mediterranean region today. First, grain heads were cut off, gathered into piles, and bound into sheaves. Next, the men loaded these sheaves onto donkeys to be carried to the threshing floor, where they were thrown down and trampled by oxen. This process threshed, or separated, the heavier heads of grain from the lighter chaff so that it could be winnowed, that is, tossed into the air with large scoops, allowing the wind to carry away the chaff and leave the grain behind. Heads of farming households then distributed the gathered grain among their farming families according to how many sheaves each had brought to the threshing floor. Then farm families would take the opportunity to rest, repair their tools, and await the next sign of inundation, sometimes within days of harvest.

Since the Egyptian year was 365 days long and the three seasons occupied 360 of these, a short five days' respite from the work was their only downtime. The annual cycle of Akhet, Peret, and Shemu defined Egyptians' existence and depended for its clockwork regularity upon the ability of its citizens to predict the inundation of the Nile which sustained them. So dependent were they on the inundation that any severe or prolonged reduction in the river's flow that occurred throughout the Old Kingdom (Bell, 1970) and likely through some or all of the First Intermediate Period, spelled economic, social, and political disaster.

**Scribes**

Given the enormous size of Egypt's government and religious bureaucracies, it is no surprise that the category of the scribe is second only to that of farmers in size. Scribes were employed on many levels, both in the public and private sectors, and were thereby exposed to opportunities for advancement. Those who worked as freelancers would sell their services to local patrons or priests. In contrast, others more fortunate could find lower-level government positions that held the possibility of promotion depending upon the scribe's skill. Because their training involved advanced courses in mathematics and basic building practices, they could be employed in government building projects, such as characterized the Early Kingdom or 'age of the pyramids,' indeed a productive time at all levels of trade and commerce. Unlike that of farmers, the schedules of scribes were dictated more by their patrons on an as-needed basis.

Once a scribe had completed his training, he was allowed to wear the uniform of a scribe: a long skirt instead of the traditional kilts of other professions. He would also be seen carrying a stone palette with two carved depressions which served as inkpots, one black and the other red, and writing brushes to perform his duties. The function of the two colors of the ink becomes quite apparent by analogy with another document. For example, you may be familiar with specific editions of the Judeo Christian Bible, which highlight the words of Christ in red while the bulk of the biblical text is printed in black. Egyptian scribes used black ink for body text and red for chapter headings or highlighting a pertinent word or phrase. A perfect example of this is the "Hymn to the Nile Flood," written on papyrus in Middle Egyptian, presumably during the Middle Kingdom Period (Hymn to the Nile flood, 2002). The scribe who recorded the lyrics used red ink for the first words of the first verse, which comprise the title, "Hymn to Hapy." The rest of the verse is written in black ink. Successive stanzas display this same distinction.

All scribal duties were predicated upon one crucial condition: The scribe-to-be must be literate. Masters expended great effort teaching their apprentices the minutiae of writing hieroglyphics. Once a student had successfully learned the Egyptian language in its hieroglyphic form, he still had two other forms, more cursive than pictorial, to learn. As with any acquired skill, tremendous effort produced better results and more significant opportunities. Mediocrity in learning the written Egyptian language consigned the overtly successful scribe to a life of humble clerking and accounting duties. Achievers could envision a future more attractive and even more lucrative than that of their average classmates.

## Craftsmen

It was essential for the craftsman working in Egyptian society to find pleasure and pride in what he produced, for society afforded him little respect. He could not read like the scribe. His products couldn't feed multitudes or fill the green storage bins of the Egyptian people. The tools with which he worked were rudimentary, and yet, with those tools, he could make precious works of art, some of which have survived to this day. Craftsmanship was most often carried out under a system of patronage. The crafting of jewelry, statues, or other works of art required a supply of raw materials out of the reach of an independent craftsman. The most precious jewels and metals were reserved for the pharaoh and his government officials. Private patrons or estates could hire an artisan on an ad hoc basis to create a particular piece of art or jewelry; patrons would be responsible for providing the raw materials for their projects and accommodation, food, and the like. Some artisans were fortunate enough to be taken on permanently and were employed full-time by their patrons. The quality of their lives depended upon the goodwill of their patron, and patrons had the right to demand time and effort from their craftsman. Under these circumstances, the lives of craftsmen were not their own. It was possible, in theory, for an artisan in an unsatisfactory patronage relationship to seek out another patron, but chances were not always suitable for success in that venture.

Artisans learned craftsmanship in an apprentice/master relationship. No instruction manuals existed because the knowledge required to know the trade was securely in the mind of the master. The work of artisans was usually passed from father to son through successive generations. Once the sun had attained the appropriate skill level, he was obligated to make his way and, hopefully, secure a good patron or a good position. The most fortunate craftsman in Egyptian society ended up working for the royal court, where their working conditions and the supply of raw materials was exemplary. But like the pyramids themselves, the opportunities for such positions at the top were smaller than at the bottom.

## Businessmen

Business people occupy a smaller proportion of the working population in Egypt than in other trades and professions. In large part, this was because the wealthy could afford their own workshops and buy their materials so that they did not need the goods of independent businessmen. There was little left over to barter in the local marketplace for lower-income clients, who had barely enough to provide for their own needs. Nor could independent business people exchange goods with foreign visitors since that avenue of trade was entirely under the control of central government agencies and their brokers. On the whole, it was not a profession with any kind of job and economic security.

## Quarrymen and Miners

When we gaze with awe and amazement at the achievements of Egypt, in particular, the glorious monuments of the Early Kingdom, known today as the Age of the Pyramids, it would be easy to lavish praise on the builders and architects who devised and designed these wonders, who orchestrated supply chains and the building of pyramid towns such as the one at the foot of the Giza plateau, or who coordinated the efforts of tens of thousands of workers from all over the Nile Valley, for twenty years of non-stop production.

These workers deserve their share of praise. But then I think of these statistics for the Great Pyramid of Khufu: 2,300,000 blocks of limestone, averaging 2 tons in weight, to be moved into place on successive courses, dressed, then positioned at the rate of one block every two minutes, 10 hours per day, seven days a week, over 7,300 or more days. Even if crews worked shifts of several days with rest days in between, the work must have been crushing. Do many hands make light work under such circumstances?

It is telling that there are no records (of which I'm aware) of the numbers of quarrymen who suffered heat stroke, broken or mangled limbs, back injuries, or death at the lowest levels of the production hierarchy. Given the nature of this and many other building projects in the glory days of ancient Egypt, quarrymen were essential workers. No limestone equals no building. Yet their tools were rudimentary, barely sufficient for the magnitude of their responsibilities. Yes, the limestone they quarried was of the softer variety, unlike that which supported the foundations of the pyramids. Still, their chisels were made of copper or bronze, the edges of which were quickly dulled, likewise the points of their picks. Lucky quarrymen worked the open pits to free their massive blocks, only to watch their counterparts have to pull them up the slope of the plateau on sleds and move them up the courses of the pyramid.

Quarrymen did all this work, day after day, for 20 years, under the harsh and unforgiving Eye of Ra, a scorching sun in a country with no clouds nor any rain. The 'resurrection machines' of the pharaohs could rightly be considered monumental tributes to the workers who risked their lives only to disappear into the sands of time.

**Herders**

Since the introduction of domestic livestock to the Nile Valley in the sixth millennium BCE, herders have occupied a vital role in the economy of the Egyptian people. The description of their job bears little difference to that of a herdsman in our day: Some cared for smaller herds on farm estates, their own or others while larger herds were attended by more nomadic herdsmen who roamed the plains with thousands of cattle, sheep, and goats. These herdsmen lived and moved with their herds: watching out for predators, seeking fresh pastoring areas and water sources, and tending to injured animals. And like the ranchers and herders of our day, roundups, last sewing, and branding were the herders' stock in trade. Briar and Hobbes point out another similarity with our day: Cattle were branded on the right shoulder to identify their owners. The only difference? The brand was in hieroglyphics!

**Marshmen**

Marshmen, it seems, were the unsung heroes and free spirits of ancient Egypt. Their privilege was to gather precious papyrus, the nation's national vegetation, from the papyrus marshes of the Delta, which they called Mohit. Almost one-third of Egypt was covered with water throughout the year, providing plenty of work and shelter for this unique niche of the working population. Their work outfit consisted of little more than a loincloth or, in some cases, no clothing at all.

Papyrus was a vital national commodity, given that all official writing was inscribed on its pages. In addition to providing the raw materials for elite scribal work, papyrus could also be used to manufacture the boats used by marshmen and for their homes. Stocks of papers could be lashed together at specific links to form a lightweight craft that marshmen could pole through the papyrus thickets. Those same bundles of papyrus bound together and patched with mud became the walls and roofs of their homes. Papyrus stems grew to upwards of 10 feet high. Marshmen could pull their boats through the thickets, cutting the papyrus stalks below the waterline, stacking them, and bundling them for personal or commercial use. If the papyrus were destined to become writing material, the bundles would be delivered to papermakers who sliced the stems lengthwise into thin strips; cut the fibers into roughly one foot lengths; and then layered them in alternating horizontal and vertical directions.

The stacks of papers were beaten with a wooden mallet, compressing the fibers and extruding their juices which, when dry, formed a kind of glue that held the layers together, producing a fine writing surface for the scribes. To finish their work the scribes trimmed the edges of the sheets and smoothed them with a polishing stone. Individual sheets could be glued together to form scrolls. In addition to papyrus harvesting, marshmen enjoyed the freedom to hunt and fish in the marshlands of the Delta. What a contrast to the narrow economy and precarious position of an Egyptian businessman!

# Chapter 3: Gods and Goddesses

Egyptian religion didn't germinate from the literary creations of some great author such as Homer, as did the religion of the Greeks, or from a syncretistic process of assimilation such as that of the Roman empire, which adopted the gods of the conquered and Latinized them. Instead, with the possible exception of Sumerian religion and Mesopotamian culture, the development of the Egyptian religion follows an entirely original trajectory: it developed directly and organically out of the human evolutionary process known as the Cognitive Revolution.

However, as *H. erectus* moved away from the trees to walk upright on the Savannah, it likely shared the primitive characteristics of its primate forebears (think of chimpanzees living in troops, caring for their young, asserting dominance, and demonstrating the hierarchical organization which enabled them to survive and to thrive). Still, at this early stage, there is no evidence of ritual, certainly not of religion. *H. heidelbergensis*, a likely descendant of *H. erectus*, demonstrated developed tactical and survival skills, the refinements in tool manufacture and hunting skills, and advances related to the ability to coordinate survival efforts within the larger community: the building of 'group homes,' rudimentary wood and hide shelters with hearths to control fire, to cook, to warm themselves against the cold, to protect against predators. These abilities were evidenced on the north coast of the Mediterranean Sea as early as 400,000 BCE (Terra Amata (archaeological site), 2021) at precisely the same time as their siblings roamed southern and eastern Africa. From a grave dated to around that time unearthed in what is now Germany, there is a suggestion of the first evidence of ritual behavior by *H. heidelbergensis*. Thirty bodies were thrown into a pit, together with several artifacts and one well-crafted, double-edged hand ax (Smithsonian's National Museum of Natural History, 2010).

The digging of a pit to inter human remains, rather than simply to leave them to the natural processes of decay and predation, may seem of little consequence. But, as we begin to see from those pit burials unearthed around the Nile Valley in the mesolithic and particularly in the Neolithic period, by which time early *Homo sapiens* had arrived on the scene, there is a progression in ritual connected to the internment of human remains which leads directly to the complex burial rituals and, yes, to the pyramids of historical Egypt.

We will return to this subject in chapter 7, discussing Egyptian burial practices and the building of the pyramids, and in chapter 8, when we unravel the mysterious process of mummification. But here is one tantalizing hint of the direction in which *Homo* was moving in prehistoric Egypt: Many of the buried remains thus far uncovered were found in shallow pits, in a contracted or fetal position, lying on their left side, head pointing to the south and facing to the west. Why so intentional a burial regimen? This question intrigues us. It beckons us to get inside the head of those who cared for their buried dead in such a purposeful, if obscure, way. Some bodies were wrapped, or at least covered, with hides or, in the early Neolithic period, with woven mats or both (I. Shaw, 2000). *Homo neanderthalensis* was discovered to bury its dead deliberately and to leave grave markers, even flowers, on top of the graves. This was the first such ceremonial behavior in the *Homo* family tree (Smithsonian's National Museum of Natural History, 2010). The earliest known mummy associated with Egyptian culture was a young *Homo sapiens* female "wrapped in linen and fur" who died around 3500 BCE (Geggel, 2017). She was buried more than 300 years before Menes/Narmur conquered the northern kingdom, taking the Red Crown of Upper Egypt and the White Crown of Lower Egypt as the first historical ruler of the unified country.

Likely by the time our young, linen-and-fur-wrapped lady was buried, and before the creation of that unifying government under Narmur in 3150 BCE, Egypt possessed, according to Bob Brier, "all the characteristics of a country except one" (Brier & A Hoyt Hobbs, 2013, p. 10). The most significant of those characteristics (aside from strong centralized government), he implies, is that the Egyptian people "spoke a common language and shared similar religious beliefs" (Brier & A Hoyt Hobbs, 2013, p. 10). Though we can, of course, infer the existence of verbal communication, and possibly some primitive form of language from the physiology of the hominid (pre-Sapiens), remains discovered thus far in the Nile Valley, it was the Cognitive Revolution which set *Homo sapiens* apart from its predecessors, according to Yuval Harari (Harari, 2014). Our species was able to coordinate its efforts, to work collaboratively, and to communicate effectively on a scale impossible for its smaller-brained predecessors to achieve and, ultimately, to dominate the entire world. We'll unpack Harari's claims later in this and the following chapter because they hold the key to our understanding of how stone-age people such as the Egyptians could establish a civilization that endured and thrived far longer than any other since.

For the first time, humans could give voice to more than the immediate, concrete facts of daily life—how to recognize an edible plant, where to locate a herd of gazelle or giant buffalo, when to light a fire for warmth or how to fashion a flint into a hand-ax. They could appreciate the abstract and the intangible, and grapple with ideas of past and future, not merely the present moment. *H. sapiens* could frame universal questions of existence, such as: where did we come from? Why does such-and-such happen? What happens when we die?

The answers they came up with and the stories which framed those answers, shared around the hearth-fire after a day of hunting or whispered to a child as they lay on their sleeping mat under a warm fur blanket or intoned at the graveside of a departed elder–these answers and these stories became the vessels for an emerging Egyptian worldview, in which the gods and their interaction with man and his world were foundational to human existence. We will read some of the essential stories in chapter 5. Now, from our vantage point of five millennia of history, we call these stories myths. But to the Egyptian people, from serf to Pharaoh and everywhere between, these stories described the most profound and significant realities. If we are to appreciate these stories as did the ancient Egyptian people, we must set aside our modern-day perspectives and prejudices and try to see the world as they might have seen it. As we do, we will come face to face with what Bob Brier has labeled the "great paradox of ancient Egypt" (Brier & A Hoyt Hobbs, 2013).

## The Great Paradox of Ancient Egypt

In the introduction to their book, *Ancient Egypt: Everyday Life in the Land of the Nile* (2013), Bob Brier and Hoyt Hobbs enumerate some of the multitudes of accomplishments that exemplify ancient Egyptian culture, from engineering and architecture to strong government and military might, from clothing and diet to medicine and art. Then they make this bold and insightful statement: "Their buildings, architecture, clothing, food, and medicine may have been thousands of years ahead of their time, but their view of the world was closer to a prehistoric caveman's than to ours" (Brier & A Hoyt Hobbs, 2013).

It seems from that statement that Brier and Hobbs find the crux of their paradox in the primitive nature of the Egyptian worldview rather than in the magnitude of their accomplishments. However, we want to turn that thinking on its head! Instead of asking how a civilization boasting of such accomplishments as Egypt has produced could be so primitive in its worldview, we should ask ourselves how the Egyptian civilization, birthed directly out of the New Stone Age and retaining her Neolithic mindset, could achieve the precocious marvels for which she is known. The answer to that question may very well be the key to understanding how this precocious, infant civilization endured well beyond any other in history. For clues to that answer, we will look, in a moment, to Yuval Noah Harari and his discussion of the power of stories (Harari, 2014).

We have seen previously how the unified nation of Egypt sprang, seemingly fully formed, from the evolutionary river of the Paleolithic and Neolithic eras. There was no Nilotic civilization that existed before Egypt and from which it could arise. There was no science to inform and explain the Egyptians' world (Brier & A Hoyt Hobbs, 2013, p. 43). But the occurrence of natural phenomena demanded an explanation. If that explanation were not visible and apparent to the watching eye, then it must be invisible—invisible and powerful. The welcome and sometimes deadly heat of the sun, or the desirable but sometimes disastrous arrival of the inundation, must be the manifestation of some hidden agency. It was not a great leap for people to ascribe the workings of nature to powerful, unseen deities.

The inhabitants of the Nile Valley were recent descendants of those who chose to settle while others of their species departed, with all or most of their Neanderthal cousins, in the Out-of-Africa migration around 65,000 BCE. Geographically isolated, and insulated at first from any significant outside cultural influence by the pre-existing cultures of the Fertile Crescent, the People of the Black Soil entered history as those "who looked both forward and back," manifesting "a paradoxical combination of startlingly modern accomplishments with incredibly ancient thought processes" (Brier & A Hoyt Hobbs, 2013, p. 2). Of these ancient thought processes, Brier and Hobbs write:

They saw the universe as inhabited by a panoply of gods–spirits that controlled every natural phenomenon and left an Egyptian feeling powerless, dependent on prayers and offerings to entice gods to accomplish what he could not do on his own. Rather than individuals pursuing their own destiny, ancient Egyptians acted like helpless pets waiting for whatever their masters, the gods, might provide (Brier & A Hoyt Hobbs, 2013).

At the zenith of their civilization, the Egyptian people collectively worshipped as many as 1,000 gods and goddesses—truly a panoply. Unfortunately, the scope of this book prevents us from meeting all of them. Still, in chapter five, we will have an opportunity to greet many of the lead actors later in this chapter and consider their roles in the most significant myths of Egyptian culture. Whether the Egyptians' incredibly ancient thought processes, specifically their well-developed belief in the power and unseen presence of this multitude of gods who controlled every aspect of their lives, left them feeling powerless, dependent or helpless, seems to border on conjecture. We cannot see their feelings, no matter how knowledgeable we have become regarding their civilization. What we can see is the outworking of their beliefs: the tombs and their inscriptions; monumental temples like that of the sun-god at Karnak, and lesser temples scattered throughout the land; religious literature such as the Pyramid and Coffin Texts; and the massive network of priests and religious workers who administer the rites of Egyptian religion on behalf of the people, in service to the gods and Pharaoh, god-on-earth. Despite Egypt's history of achievement followed by periods of internal strife, even civil war, and of increasing conflict with foreign aggressors, Egyptian civilization's single most significant galvanizing force has been its shared beliefs.

## Speech, Fiction, and the Birth of a Civilization

Earlier, we heard Brier and Hobbs speak of the emergence of Egyptian civilization at the end of the Neolithic period (c. 3150 BCE) and how it "possessed all the characteristics of a country except one," namely, a unifying central government (Brier & Hoyt Hobbs, 2013, p. 10). The victory of Narmur secured the latter. Now there may be any number of characteristics which, taken together, define a country, yet, interestingly, Brier and Hobbs enumerated only two: the speaking of a common language and the sharing of similar religious beliefs (Brier & Hoyt

Hobbs, 2013). Most fascinating is that the development of precisely these two elements–the capacity to conceive of fictions, not merely to understand concrete facts, and the ability to share them via a common language–characterizes what Yuval Noah Harari has dubbed the Cognitive Revolution of *H. sapiens.* These modern humans occurred between 70,000 BCE and 30,000 BCE (Harari, 2014). When we pull apart Harari's argument for the extraordinary, earth-changing impact of this singular evolutionary event, we'll discover the profound significance of communal belief in the gods, goddesses, myths, and traditions which inhabited the worldview of ancient Egyptian civilization.

# The Cognitive Revolution of *Homo Sapiens*

Harari makes the intriguing and straightforward observation that "beginning about 70,000 years ago, *Homo sapiens* started doing very special things" (Harari, 2014, p. 18). I can't help but imagine a slight upturn to the corner of his mouth, at the humor of such a massive understatement. Within 5,000 years or so (the blink of an eye in evolutionary time), representative modern humans would depart East Africa to take over the world! In the process, they would eradicate *H. erectus,* their evolutionary grandfather, *H. heidelbergensis*, their father, and *H. neanderthalensis,* their sibling, with whom their species had shared the planet for almost 200,000 years. Thus, a multi-species mankind would be reduced, by around 40,000 BCE, to one species: *my kind.*

The keys to this 160,000-year process of bringing the whole world under *sapiens* domination could be found in two places, that is, on their tongues and in their imaginations. As Harari says, "The appearance of new ways of thinking and communicating, between 70,000 and 30,000 years ago, constitutes the Cognitive Revolution" (2014, p. 19). The upshot of this revolution was that, for the first time, man was free to conceptualize, dream, *imagine* things beyond the empirical scope, and share these things with others.

[T]he truly unique feature of our language is not its ability to transmit information about men and lions. Rather, it's the ability to transmit information about things that do not exist at all. As far as we know, only Sapiens can talk about entire kinds of entities that they have never seen, touched, or smelled (Harari, 2014, p. 23).

Harari categorizes these "kinds of entities," including "legends, myths, gods, and religions," as types of fiction which enable us to imagine things *"collectively"* (2014, p. 23) and "to cooperate flexibly in large numbers." These fictions, he says, were the product of the Cognitive Revolution (2014, p. 24). Putting aside for the moment Harari's atheistic bias, we might ask the question, at what point in time did modern humans living in the Nile Valley first begin to entertain the fiction of a divine realm, populated with such a diverse and colorful cast of characters as the gods and goddesses of Egypt? How and with whom did they share their stories? We can never know for sure. If we were to use our imagination, however, we might soon find ourselves sitting quietly inside a fringe of warm hearth-glow, where a young father stirs ashen embers with a pointed stick. At the same time, the mother speaks in hushed tones to the child sitting in her lap, blanketed with furs and wrapped snugly in her arms. She has been telling story after story of those very gods and goddesses. If we listen carefully, we might be able to hear some of those stories for ourselves. Let's listen, then...

# The Gods of Chaos

## The Ogdoad

Let me tell you about the Eightfold, or Ogdoad, who existed from primordial times and were worshipped from antiquity. The Ogdoad was a group of primordial gods and goddesses who embodied the qualities or characteristics of the primordial chaos from which arose the *benben*, or primeval mound of creation. The word primordial refers to a time before time and space, an indefinite period before the world's creation. The central location for their worship was initially called Eight Town but was later changed to Hermopolis Magna (Pinch, 2004). The Eightfold is therefore often referred to as the Ogdoad of Hermopolis. The Ogdoad consisted of four male deities and their female counterparts, each pair representing a particular quality of the primordial chaos. Bob Brier maintains that, concerning myths and the deities they involve, we know that they are not meant to be taken literally, but we can understand the realities they represent (Brier, 1999). So, for example, one of the divine pairs of the Ogdoad is the god Nun and his counterpart Nunet, who personify the primordial waters out of which the mound arose.

Amun, whose name means the Hidden One, and Amunet, his female counterpart, likely represent the formlessness of the primordial state. Amun was sometimes described as part of the Eightfold and as the one who brought the eight into existence together with the world. When he and Amunet are absent from the Eightfold, their place is most frequently occupied by the divine pair, Nia and Niat, representing the primordial void from which all things sprang. Kek and Keket embody darkness. Notice the striking parallel between this personified description of the primordial chaos and that of the Judeo-Christian creation account: "Now the earth was formless and void, and darkness was upon the face of the waters" (Gen. 1:2, KJV). The Ogdoad was either represented in temple carvings in human form or else with the males having frog heads and the females, snake heads. According to Geraldine Pinch, "the Ogdoad seem to be forces that the creator has to subdue before the work of creation can begin. In others, they simply seem to die after bringing forth life" (Pinch, 2004).

## The Creator Gods

### Amun and Amunet

Amun, the creator god, is portrayed as either one of the Ogdoad of Hermopolis or as the creator god of the Eightfold. In his capacity as creator, he stands apart from, and exercises his power over, the qualities of chaos represented by the four pairs of gods he speaks into existence at the beginning of creation. When Atum is depicted in the role of the creator god, Amun and Amunet form the fourth pair, representing headedness or invisibility of the primordial chaos. His origins are somewhat obscure. In the Pyramid Texts Amun and Amunet are divine protectors of the king. Amun was the chief God of the Theban religion by the Middle Kingdom, believed to rule as a divine pharaoh from his cult temple at

Karnak. His new consort there was named Mut and his son Khonsu. Unlike other Egyptian gods, Amun was not tethered to any locality or even to a divine realm. Instead, Egyptians imagined him as omnipresent, close at hand, and ready to aid his human children, be they pharaohs or servants. He seemed, in a sense, to be more approachable and involved in the lives of his creation.

Amun was most often portrayed as a bearded man in the prime of life. Later, in the New Kingdom, mythology brought his latent virility to the forefront. Amun was purported to unite sexually with the queen of Egypt to produce divine-human offspring. Amun may have been linked with the ram during the Middle Kingdom to embody male virility and sexual potency. When united with the sun god Ra, Amun became the originator of all life. Perhaps, though, his name is most familiar to our ears as the latter part of the name of one of the most famous pharaohs in our western experience: Tutankhamun!

## Atum

Atum, whose name means completion or totality, is the preeminent deity among the Ennead, or Nine, of Heliopolis. Atum is the first of gods, the Self-Created, having risen from the surrounding waters with the *benben*, or primordial mound. Alone and lonely, Atum is said to have masturbated and then swallowed his semen, creating two offspring, the twins Shu and Tefnut. Atum is depicted as representing the setting sun. Egyptians believed him to embody the potential for all life.

## Ra, the Sun God

It is entirely straightforward to characterize Ra, god of the sun: all that the Egyptian people perceived the sun over their heads to be, and to do, are the most apparent characteristics of Ra himself. The sun is the bringer of light, and the giver of life, particularly to the crops planted out of the inundation which depended upon it to bring them to fruition. Without the light of the sun, men could not work to feed their families and their animals. Without its heat, they would suffer, even perish. The regular appearance of the sun at dawn and its setting at dusk represented the order of Maat which pushed away chaos and gave security to the Egyptian people. As it traveled from horizon to horizon, it dominated the upper sky and was the brightest light therein, outshining all other lights. The sun traveled in its visible arc across the upper sky, which was the realm of Horus. So Ra became associated in the people's minds with Horus and was called Ra of Horus of the Two Horizons. He was sometimes depicted with the body of a man and the head of a falcon, representing Horus, crowned with a coiled cobra. The cobra imagery represents the Eye of Ra, which looks down upon the earth, and the manifestation of Horus himself, whose two eyes are said to be the sun and the moon.

The Eye of Ra also had a negative connotation under certain circumstances. For example, when the Nile failed to rise and the land became parched, the unmerciful Eye of Ra could be seen above, sending its scorching heat to cause famine and death. It would have been difficult for the Egyptian people not to infer from Ra's divine judgment for their sins and failures. Their mythology already contained stories of Ra sending forth his eye to exact punishment upon his creatures who were said to be created from the tears of that same Eye.

The cyclical journey of Ra, the visible sun, over the earth, across the upper sky, and through the Underworld, Duat, every 24 hours evidenced his power and rule over all creation. Ra, therefore, came to be understood as the greatest of all gods. The rise of the sun cult toward the end of the Early Kingdom was a tacit acknowledgement of this shift in Ra's status. The pharaohs increasingly sought to identify with Ra instead of Horus to bolster their claims to divinity by the end of the Fifth Dynasty. This tradition continued throughout the rest of ancient Egyptian history. Thus, Pharaoh came to be regarded as the son of Ra, ruling with the absolute power of his divine Father.

**Ptah**

Ptah was a vital creator God of Egyptian mythology whose worship was centered in the Egyptian capital of Memphis. The city of Memphis in ancient times radiated outward from the central temple of Ptah. The image of Ptah was that of a bearded man with beautiful blue skin, wearing an artisan's cap and cloak. He carried a scepter whose symbols combined the ideas of dominion, stability, and life. He was said to bestow these on the pharaohs, often crowned at his temple in Memphis.

Ptah was said to have made the world with his heart and his tongue, the heart being the center of thought and purpose and the tongue, the instrument of power, speaking a word that made things come to be. By the Middle Kingdom era, Ptah's creative power as a divine craftsman gave him the ability to craft the bodies of humans and the new bodies of the dead. Ptah was recognized as the patron of metalworkers and sculptors. Ptah was intimately linked to Osiris and, by extension, the Egyptian mummification process. In the Middle Kingdom and later, spells and incantations were inscribed inside the lids of the coffins of the deceased as helps in the afterlife. These were appropriately called 'Coffin Texts.' One of these Coffin Texts relates how Ptah helped Horus to break open the mouth of Osiris so that he could breathe. This event had its practical counterpart in the opening of the mouth ceremony performed at every funeral for the people of Egypt. One of the last steps in the ceremony was performed by a priest of Ptah who, using a small silver instrument, symbolically opened the mouth of the mummified deceased by touching the lips and reciting a prayer over the body. This last and most important right of burial could only be performed and orchestrated by a priest of Ptah.

Later conceptions of Ptah, such as in Memphite theology, position him as the self-created creator. He made everything with his heart and tongue. That is, his thoughts and speech. Ptah has also been associated with the Ogdoad, particularly Nun and Nunet, which gave birth to Atum. Ptah is similarly portrayed as taking the place of Shu in the separation of earth and sky to open up a space for creation to occur.

## Khnum

Khnum was usually depicted as a man with the head of a longhorn ram. Khnum was responsible for the creation of human and animal bodies and giving them life and health. He was often portrayed sitting at a potter's wheel crafting the bodies. This divine creation of human and animal life was understood not as an event never to be repeated. It was an ongoing process for Khnum to craft human and animal life all the time, every day. His work is never done.

Khnum was believed to control the inundation, and he personified the life-giving force of the annual flood. He was a chief God of the First Cataract adjacent to Elephantine Island beneath which, people believed, were twin caverns containing the inundation water.

# The Created Gods: the Ennead of Heliopolis

## Shu

Shu is one of the twin offspring of Atum and one of the nine primordial gods of the Ennead of Heliopolis. He is often depicted wearing a feather on his head. Shu is the god of dry air and sunlight who separates the earth from the upper sky. After Atum had masturbated and then swallowed his own semen to recreate himself, he sneezed out Shu and spat out his twin sister

Tefnut. After Shu had sex with his sister, she gave birth to two children: Geb, god of the earth, and Nut, goddess of the sky. When Shu later discovered his children, Geb and Nut, locked in a passionate embrace, he separated them. That act of separating the sky above from the earth below opened up a space that enabled creation to proceed.

## Tefnut

Tefnut is "the greatly beloved daughter" (Pinch, 2004, p. 197) of Atum and the twin sister and sexual partner of her brother Shu. Tefnut may have some association with moisture, perhaps the morning dew, according to Pinch (2004, p. 196). She has the distinction of having given birth to Geb, god of the earth, and Nut, goddess of the sky, whom their father Shu was forced to separate because of their physical indiscretions.

## Geb

Geb is a pivotal figure in Egyptian mythology. God of the earth, Geb, is the son of Tefnut by her brother-mate Shu and brother of Nut, goddess of the sky. Geb and his sister-mate Nut represent the third generation of divinities that comprise the Ennead of Heliopolis. The forcible separation of Geb from his sister Nut while they were in each other's arms has given rise to one of the iconic creation stories of Egyptian mythology. Despite their interrupted passion, Gen and Nut became the parents of five of the most important divinities of Egyptian myth: Osiris, Isis, Nephthys, Horus the elder, and Seth. Geb was often depicted as human in keeping with his preeminent role as God of the earth. His skin was occasionally painted green to represent the vegetation that springs from the world, and he personifies the ground upon which living creatures can crawl.

Geb was considered the leader of the Ennead and the king of all kings of the earth. To be a pharaoh was to sit on Geb's throne, a position of absolute earthly power (Pinch, 2004).

**Nut**

Nut is the goddess of the sky, the sister-mate of Geb, and the daughter of Shu, God of the air, and Tefnut, his mate. She is frequently depicted as a naked woman, her body stretched arch-like over the earth, just as is our sky. Though separated from her brother and mate, Geb, Nut gives birth to five of the most significant deities in the Egyptian pantheon. The drama of these five siblings is pivotal to our appreciation of Egyptian mythology and the establishment and governing of the nation of Egypt in the time of the pharaohs. We will consider these five and their complex inter-relationship in the next chapter. The role of Nut is pivotal to mythological explanations of the rising and setting of the sun and moon and the appearance of the stars in the night sky. I appreciate the imagery of the role of Nut within the created order as outlined by Pinch below:

In the day, the sun god sailed along the "sea below the belly of Nut." Each evening, the sun god was swallowed by Nut and passed through a perilous inner sky inside her. At dawn, Nut gave birth to the sun, her blood turning the sky red. At the same time, she would be swallowing the moon and the stars to give birth to them again at dusk (Pinch, 2004, p. 174).

## Osiris

The myth of Osiris and Isis may very well be the most important in all of Egyptian mythology. Their story is as banal and as bloody as any late-night drama. Yet the lessons it teaches or, perhaps, the questions it was crafted to answer are among the most fundamental questions of human existence. What happens to us when we die? Oh, that is the first question in every generation of humankind. What happens to my body? Is there such a thing as a soul? If so, what does it look like? Will my body stay dead, or will it somehow have the chance for life again? Does my soul live after death? If so, where and how does it live? What kind of life is it that I can experience after my body dies?

I could continue asking more such questions, but I know you understand what I'm saying because, admit it, you've asked those questions yourself and more at some point in your life. No, the Egyptians lived when there were no certainties, no science, no atoms or DNA. These fundamental human questions demanded answers. It remains unclear where, when, and how Osiris became the answer to those questions. Still, sometime between the unification under Narmer and the fifth dynasty in the middle of the third millennium BC, Osiris seems to have risen to prominence in the world view of the Egyptian people. One of the earliest primary sources for the story of the birth, death, and afterlife of Osiris is the Pyramid Texts. Remember that, as with all Egyptian myths, the details can change from dynasty to dynasty and era to era. But we can speak with reasonable certainty about how Osiris was depicted. And since every aspect of Egyptian burial and mummification derives from the story of Osiris, it is no surprise that he is described as a mummified pharaoh wearing a crown and carrying a crook and flail, the traditional symbols of kingly rule and power. Portraying his skin as either green or black has been suggested by some to represent decomposition. Still, it came to be associated through his myth with the endless cycle of death and rebirth, which was integral to the Egyptian worldview.

Who was Osiris? If there were a human figure behind the story, it would be virtually impossible to determine. There is no historical evidence for an actual king or other historical figure being the first Osiris. But of the mythical Osiris, we have already learned a little in the previous chapter. Osiris was one of five children of the earth god Geb and his sister-mate Nut who, as the story goes, were discovered by their father so close together in a passionate embrace that there was no space between them. Their father, Shu, was forced to separate them as far as the upper sky is from the earth to create a space for the creation of men and creatures of the planet. Osiris and Isis, his sister-mate, ruled Egypt together until the events of the Osiris myth occurred, when his brother Seth struck him down out of jealousy, causing Isis to use her powers of magic to reanimate him. Having been resurrected by Isis, Osiris is overcome by passion and impregnates his sister, and for most Westerners, he gives birth to Horus. Horus in turn will become the God of the living while his father Osiris became the God of the Dead.

Wrapped up in the mythical person and work of Osiris are the ideas of the afterlife, judgment, truth, or Maat, as the Egyptians termed it. Moreover, the myth of Osiris is the genesis of the burial practice of mummification, which typifies Egyptian civilization from our perspective. The sarcophagus of the pharaohs is a physical representation of the wooden box designed by Seth to entomb his brother. It was a box made to the exact specifications of its inhabitant. Sealed with lead or other material, the mummification process was an extension of the Isis and Osiris mythology, which necessitated that Isis reassemble her brother-mate's dismembered body before she could reanimate it. The underlying belief contained in that story is that a body must be intact as it enters the afterlife for that body to be resurrected. The resurrection of Osiris himself is a type of experience that every Egyptian desired. Osiris is termed Lord of the Westerners. The term "westerner" refers to the deceased spirits over whom he rules in the afterlife. Resurrection has always been associated with the west in Egyptian thinking. That is why burial ceremonies bring the mummified remains of the deceased across the Nile River in a boat from east to west so that the body can be buried on the west side of the Nile.

Osiris' experience in the afterworld is also a pattern or an archetype of that experience. Every Egyptian could anticipate thorough judgment on the way to the next life. As Osiris had to face a determination of truth, each soul must undergo that same experience over which Osiris himself will preside. Those judgments determined if, in a literal sense, one's heart was true. Another way of expressing that would be the judgment of Osiris that one was a possessor of *Maat*, being the principle of truth, justice, and order in opposition to chaos, which is untruth, disorder, and injustice. With the aid of Isis, Horus, and other deities, Osiris argued his case in the Hall of Double Truth before a tribunal of 42 gods, and, as we say, he passed with flying colors. Osiris was vindicated, and his death was deemed to be unjust. For that reason, the creator God allowed Osiris to leave his mummy and reign in the underworld. He was given a new name: Wennefer. According to Pinch (p. 179), the actual raising of Osiris seems to be accomplished by Horus presenting the power of his eyes to Osiris. Though Osiris' new name was originally believed to mean "the one whose body did not decay," it later came to be understood as "the beneficent one." (Pinch, 2004).

## Isis

It is not clear from the earliest accounts of Osiris and Horus what role she played or its significance. By the New Kingdom era, however, Isis had been elevated to a position of reverence and respect, causing her to be worshipped more widely than any other Egyptian deity. That's quite impressive, given the mythological company she kept. But perhaps her elevation is entirely understandable, given that the Osiris-Isis myth depicts her as a loving and devoted wife and protective, nurturing mother. According to some texts, she will stop at nothing to avenge her husband's murder at the hands of their brother Seth. Specific texts indicate that Isis's hatred for her brother Seth is boundless and eternal. Isis was a tender mate and mother but a fierce opponent. There is much to admire about such an individual.

What do we know of Isis herself? We know that, like Osiris and Seth, she was among the five children of Geb, lord of the earth, and Nut, goddess of the upper sky. These five children represent the fourth generation in the Ennead of Heliopolis. She is typified as the throne goddess, such that the iconography of her Egyptian name is the throne symbol. In that role, she was recognized as the mother of every Egyptian king. Isis is portrayed furthermore as having the same maternal tenderness for humanity that she does for her children, Horus, and, by extension, for all of humankind. It would have been hard not to love her! What is interesting about the position of Isis is that her mythology grew up amid a male-dominated, patriarchal society. There were comparatively few female pharaohs throughout the history of Egypt, and yet, over them all, this remarkable woman, wife, and mother reigned. I wonder at the parallels between this god-mother and mother of a god and another more familiar to our western experience, the Mary of Catholic tradition, which is titled "Mother of God." She sits on a throne in the heavens presiding over God's representative on earth, his vicar, the pope. But that's just speculation and not germane to our Study.

Some Egyptian texts emphasize the power of Isis to work magic and highlight her cleverness, cunning and determination. By the later New Kingdom, a cult had developed around the person of Isis, which honored her as the guide and guardian of sailors, the inventor of agriculture, and the giver of the blessing of the annual inundation. It is not difficult to see how Isis could become the center of the Egyptian worldview and religion.

## Seth

Does every family have a black sheep? If that were true, the divine family would be no exception. Seth is the bad boy brother of Osiris, Horus the Elder, Isis, and Nephthys, and a fourth-generation member of the Ennead of Heliopolis. He is described as tumultuous and thoughtless, portrayed as a brute with incredible strength, like the enforcer in a powerful and dysfunctional family. The cult of Seth seems to have originated in upper Egypt (Pinch 192). In the early dynastic period of Egypt, Seth was alternatively identified with the gods of the despised Redland, the eastern desert, and Western Sahara. Dangerous desert conditions and wild animals were associated with the presence and activity of Seth. He is depicted as an unsavory imaginary creature. Egyptians believed him to masquerade as various animals, all of them destructive in one way or another.

Seth is a god of perpetual strife, conflict, and jealousy, whose battles with Horus are represented in several Egyptian sources. But, of course, Seth is perhaps best known for his pivotal role in the unfolding drama of Osiris and Isis. In that central myth, Seth is the deceiver and the murderer of his brother Osiris. Seth is, in this way, a catalyst for the cycle of death and rebirth and, like the antiheroes of other fictions, is acknowledged as necessary to move the plot forward, in this case, to a happy ending. Without Seth, one might say that there would have been no Osiris the resurrected Lord of the Westerners. And so, while it is easy to dislike the character of Seth, we recognize that we can't disown him from the family. We can undoubtedly resonate with his sister's hatred for him. So what is the reality behind Seth? There's no way that we can say for sure. All we can do is think about the possible questions that his character will answer. I suggest, perhaps, that one of those questions that ring true in every generation on earth is: Why do horrible things happen to good people? That seems an appropriate question, and Seth, the deceiver, seems like a reasonable answer, at least to the Egyptian mind.

## Nephthys

In how many stories do we have two siblings, one of whom is accomplished, beautiful, and famous while the other is inconspicuous? Are we growing up in the shadow of our beloved sibling? That story seems as old as time. And, yes, it is the story of Nephthys and her sister Isis, the throne goddess. Isis would have been a tough act to follow, and it seems Nephthys knew this. She is mainly portrayed as a devoted sister but a woman of little significance and few accomplishments. If the Pyramid Texts indicate her status, then to describe her as "an imitation woman with no vagina" (Pinch, 2004, p. 171) is probably the worst insult one could level. By today's standards, she was a spinster who, having been raped by her brother Seth, chose to move in with Osiris and Isis. The pictorial representation of her name represents "lady of the manor." According to some texts, she slept with the Lord of the Manor, Osiris, much to Isis' chagrin, and gave birth to Anubis, with whom many will be familiar even if they know little about Egyptian mythology. Anubis, the jackal-headed god, is the master of the dead and oversees the embalming and burial rights of Egyptian practice.

Nephthys, the devoted sister, shared with her sister Isis searching for their brother, Isis' mate, Osiris. After finding the body, Isis and Nephthys were on hand while Anubis mummified their brother's body. Nephthys is associated with the linens used for wrapping the mummified body since she is recognized as one of the goddesses of weaving. Nephthys and her sister Isis were portrayed as the protectors of the mummified corpse of their brother and later came to typify the gods' protection over the remains of the dead.

**Horus**

We must distinguish at the outset between two Horuses. There is the child Horus, the son of Isis by her brother-mate Osiris; and the Horus of whom we speak now, the Elder, the brother of Seth against whom he engaged in constant struggle. The falcon represented this elder Horus, the lord of the sky, whose wings spanned heaven and whose two eyes were the sun and the moon. In this capacity, Egyptians believed him to be the child of a sky goddess, either Nut or Hathor. Egypt's earliest kings were frequently typified as hawks praying on their enemies, an allusion to the role of Horus, the embodiment of pharaoh's rule. Some parts of the mythical cycle describe a time when the gods ruled directly on earth. In these, the reign of Horus is seen as the perfect paradigm of earthly rule, the pattern and prototype for future pharaonic reign.

The rulers of the Early Dynastic Period sometimes took as many as four "Horus names" for their official designations to identify the attributes for which they most desired to be remembered. They included the symbol of Horus in the glyphs, which represented their public names. Pharaohs of later dynasties moved away from identification with Horus to embrace the cult of the sun god Ra, of whom they claimed to be the sons (or daughters, in some cases), and therefore divine.

## Horus, the Child

Horus, the child, is the son of Isis, conceived by her brother and mate Osiris after his reanimation and given birth to after his father's descent into the underworld to reign there as Lord of the Westerners. Horus, the child, is, strangely enough, portrayed as a young Egyptian boy, naked, his head shaved save for one braided side lock. When shown as the third member of divine triads in mini temples throughout Egypt, he is the preeminent one. His role as child-god is to represent the renewal of the world. The birth of a child heralds hope for the future, and so must Horus the child have been recognized. And the pregnancy of Isis was said to have been ten months along, and her delivery exceptionally difficult and painful. Isis was forced to hide little Horus in the papyrus thickets of the Nile delta to protect him from his uncle Seth.

Images of the innocent Horus child were especially appealing to the pharaohs who acknowledged their dependence upon the gods in the same way that an infant depended on his mother for protection, nourishment, and growth.

# Chapter 4: Myth and Mythology of Ancient Egypt

## Toward a Worldview

Let's indulge in a thought experiment. Let's think back to our childhood, wherever and whenever that was, before the invasion of digital media, google, iPads and cell phones, and the Hubble space telescope. For some of us, that's a long journey, and for others, just a few short steps. If you were born after Apple and Microsoft windows, you might find this experiment a challenge. No matter. Now try to remember the first time you stood outside late on a clear night and gazed up at the sky. Are you with me? Questions were bouncing around inside your head, weren't they? Questions like: Where did all this come from? What are those lights in the sky and how did they get there? You look around and ask yourself: How did this get here? Mommy, and daddy, and crazy aunt Edna who could never fail to pinch your cheek every time she saw you. How did they–how did I–get here? And those are just a handful of all the questions that you and I have. Now imagine for a moment and ask yourself this question: What if there was no one and nothing in my world to which I could turn for the answers? No Wikipedia, no Google search, no science at all. Don't imagine, at this point, that you know these things exist but that you simply don't have access to them. Instead, imagine that these things don't exist at all.

Could you do it? Well, then, congratulations! You've just experienced, for the briefest moment, what it was like at every moment of every day, for each man, woman, and child walking this narrow strip of Black Land as the Stone Age gave way to the Pyramid Age.

You are that late Neolithic child, looking around at your world, your head filled with those questions we've asked ourselves. Life is ok, you guess, but not easy. Father came back today looking sad, only two fish in his fishing basket.

The nearby river that was so full last summer that it took away your little brother is now so low that you can almost cross it without getting your knees wet. And little water means no black dirt. Mother's garden looks dry, and nothing wants to grow. Father turns his face to the sun, and his face is angry. The bright, hot sun looks angry too. What can you do? Do you feel helpless? Afraid? You ask father why this is happening to us, but all he can say is, "I don't know."

"Why are there no more fish?"

"I don't know."

"When will the black dirt come back so mother's garden can make more to eat?"

"I don't know."

"Why is mother's belly getting round again? Will I get another brother?"

"Go ask your mother."

Our *H. sapiens* brains, hot-wired between 70,000 and 30,000 years ago during the Cognitive Revolution, began to think and communicate in new ways. We need to know and to understand not just some things but everything. If we don't know, if we can't know, we're inclined to fill in the blanks.

I'll bet that, before the Cognitive Revolution, our species didn't ask many questions. Concrete thinking, characterized by our *Homo* ancestors before 70,000 BCE, observes that "Todd was killed by an elephant yesterday." Post-Cognitive Revolution, that would never happen. "Why did Todd have to get stepped on by that elephant yesterday? Who is responsible for that elephant wandering into our back yard so it could kill Todd?"

Every parent has experienced the interminable questionings of their children. Their questions, we believe, require answers. When we don't know the answers–when there is no possible way to know–and when, at the same time, we must provide them, we tell stories. We fill in the blanks. We weave tales. And those stories, told and re-told, shared with other children and recounted by their parents, then passed on from generation to generation down through the ages, become the myths that characterize our times and the worldview which permeates our culture.

And so, somewhere back in time, inside a wattle-and-daub hut close to *iteru*, a little child, tucked beneath a fur blanket on her palette near the glowing hearth, looked up at her mother and asked the question: Why? And that mother began to weave a story of a time when there was only water, dark and churning, full of all the possibilities of life, and of how the Primordial Mound began to rise from the water, and sitting atop that mound, Atum, the self-created, the source of life, alone, and lonely.

## Mythology: A Moving Target

Egyptian mythology was born out of millennia of oral tradition in the late Neolithic era. Modern humans living in the Nile Valley had not yet developed a system of writing. Like many cultures, their truths and traditions were passed from fathers to their sons, mothers to their daughters, and generation to generation. These stories were memorized and recited, creating what we might think of as an oral corpus, or body of work. There was no existing method of codifying and collecting the stories of the culture we call myths today in that predynastic Egyptian culture. This reality of predynastic and dynastic Egyptian culture meant that the stories were free to change and develop over time, though fixed in their essentials. They were influenced by evolutionary, social, and political forces around them. As a result, you can find many Egyptian myths in several versions. With the unification of Egypt under King Narmur, the local myths of the villages of Upper and Lower Egypt became national myths. Over time, the events and even the names of the individuals involved morphed. Any attempt to capture Egyptian mythology in some westernized and codified way is frustrating, if not impossible. We cannot impose our Greek logic and rationality onto what is essentially an oral tribal tradition. The Greeks, by the way, had the good fortune of a prime position amid the stream of civilization: their writing was well-established. Authors such as Homer could craft their stories of Greek gods and goddesses who created the world, who controlled the movement of the planets, who hurled their lightning bolts and shook the earth, and could capture them for posterity with the stroke of a pen.

While we find it easy to pick up a volume of Greek mythology and read virtually the same stories in the exact words from many different sources, we cannot as quickly compile and organize Egyptian myths into clear and logical units. The stories were written inside the lids of coffins, on the walls of tombs and temples, in palaces and passageways and papyri over the thousand miles of monuments that comprised the Nile Valley. So we'll talk about some of these Egyptian myths in this book instead of sharing them in story form. The opportunity exists for some future Egyptian scholar, or latter-day Homer of Egyptian mythology, to gather these stories into a form that could be read by parents to their children, just as was done around the hearths of ancient Egypt. But that is not this book! Instead, I encourage you to chase some of the references from the bibliography at the end of this book and read more of the fascinating world of Egyptian mythology.

## In the Beginning...

"The origin of the universe," according to Geraldine Pinch, "was an intellectual problem that came to fascinate the Egyptians." (Pinch, 2004). Many of the gods and goddesses we've come to know in the previous chapter are directly or indirectly related to the origin of the universe and the creation of the things that constitute our world. Atum, for example, was already an ancient player in primordial creation stories by the time of the early Kingdom. While no writing exists before Narmur and his famous palette, we can infer that Atum's story comes from ancient oral tradition. Atum and the Ogdoad, or Eightfold, could read the first chapter of the Egyptian worldview in much the same way as the first chapter of the book of Genesis defines the worldview of Hebrew and Christian cultures.

We have encountered bits and pieces of this creation story in the brief biographies of its divine participants. Let's consider it now as the story unfolds. Let's remind ourselves of the perspective suggested by Bob Brier, that we do not take the stories literally but rather try to see how those stories might provide answers to the questions we ask of the world around us.

## Chaos

In our quest to decipher the intricacies of Egyptian mythology, it behooves us to remember that the non-negotiable details of that mythology, that is, the things which remain the same over time, afford us the closest glimpse into the worldview of Egyptian culture. I suggest that the one belief that undergirds Egyptian mythology, like a mathematical constant, is that before there was anything, there was *isfet*: chaos, or disorder. The Egyptian understanding of chaos provides a counterpoint to order and its pursuit, which was intrinsic to Egyptian culture. As we've seen previously, the recognition of and the striving toward order as an antidote to chaos pervades, perhaps defines, the ancient Egyptian psyche. Numerous historians have remarked that aside from what we might call microevolution in the culture of Egypt over 3000 years, from a macro view, she remained the same through that whole time. As much as the worldview of the Egyptians was tuned to the obtaining and preserving of order in their universe, it was just as much a desire to prevent a return to chaos. The history of Egypt displays this duality of thinking. A unified kingdom with its central government, religious structure, and fixed social organization came from the chaos of predynastic history. The universe demanded that life be lived by rules which upheld its internal order. When those rules and those structures were honored, the country underwent periods of stability and growth. Egyptian society maintained balance. The early Middle and New Kingdoms were evidence of the restoration of order and the maintaining of balance. The average Egyptian would perceive those times between, which historians had labeled the first, second, and sometimes third intermediate periods as times when the balance was disrupted and chaos ruled. But what is the true nature of chaos?

The Egyptian worldview saw things ordered in pairs: light and darkness, earth and sky, life and death, male and female. In this case, primordial time was when only one thing existed: Chaos. There was not yet an order to balance the universe. It would take the emergence of the creator to create that order. The word chaos evoked an image of a dark and formless infinite watery void. This was the primordial water from which all life springs. Egyptians called it Nu, or Nun. The Nu was conceived of as containing all the potential for life and existence. From the Nu, these primordial waters, the first land arose: the primordial mound, or *benben*. The primordial waters continue to surround the mound even after creation and were believed to be the ultimate source of the Nile, according to Pinch (2004). Sitting cross-legged upon the primordial mound as it arose from the chaotic primordial waters was Atum the "unique one in the Nu" and as "one who is in his egg," alone until he creates the Ogdoad, the Eightfold "by speaking with the nun" (Pinch, p.59).

Atum is understood to have created another eight gods whom we know as the Ogdoad by speaking with the Nun. These eight may represent the previously hidden elements of chaos which Atum speaks into existence, possibly by saying their names. To have one's name spoken, in Egyptian thought, was to avoid the second death in the afterlife. Some authors suggest that it is this reason that pharaohs, in particular, took for themselves several names and ensured that these names were inscribed in texts, tombs, monuments, and temples. The underlying idea is that there is power in the speaking of a name. You can read more about the

Ogdoad in the previous chapter. Often included in the Ogdoad were the gods Amun and Amunet. Amun was identified as the hidden one or the invisible. Later accounts separated Amun from the Eightfold and made him the creator God who spoke the others into existence. Different imagery exists to describe the moment of that first creation. Some sources describe that first sound as a loud cry, a heavy sigh, or even the honking of a goose. Atum/Amun is often called the creator sun god because Egyptians believed that the first appearance of the creator brought the first light and power of the sun to support life. Some accounts have a tomb cry out or whisper to drive back the primordial waters and to expose the first land, the primordial mound, to provide a place for him to begin his work.

# Creation

## The Ogdoad

The relation between the creator god Atum or Amun and the Ogdoad varies among different texts and sources. We have seen that the creator

God arose from the primordial waters simultaneously with the primordial mound and then spoke the other eight gods into existence or separated their properties from the undifferentiated chaos. Specific texts would say that the eight came together, perhaps by "some primitive instinct" (Pinch, 2004, p. 177), to make the primordial mound upon which the creator emerged. As Pinch says, "the Ogdoad merged in the primeval waters to allow the creator to come into being." This paradoxical chicken-and-egg scenario only highlights that Egyptian thinking and orientation in time were not necessarily linear. The Ogdoad could be said to be the fathers and mothers of the Creator God. And yet, it could also be noted that the creator is the father of the fathers and mothers. We should not spend much effort trying to unravel what is fixed in time over 5000 years. It should simply serve as an example of the challenge of understanding the thinking of a culture so removed in time and space from our own.

We met the Ogdoad in the previous chapter. Still, it serves our purposes to remind ourselves of the names of these dualities and the qualities or principles and body. The first pair representing the primordial waters themselves are Nun and Nunet. When included within the eight, Amun and Amunet represent the hidden or invisible within chaos and possibly the invisible breath of life. When they are absent from the eight, when creation is ascribed to Amun himself, another pair, Nia and Niat, takes their place. This pair represents the chaotic void. Kek and Keket, The third pairing represent the darkness of a chaotic state. The fourth duet is somewhat harder to identify in its characteristics, for they do not appear in most texts and sources. Finally, Tenemet or Heh as he is otherwise known, and his partner Hehet, are thought to represent chaos itself, and the strong and turbulent currents of the primordial waters, respectively.

The purpose of the Ogdoad in the process of creation seems as murky as the primordial waters themselves. Yet, this account answers the question: what was it like before there was anything? The Ogdoad, which personifies the qualities or characteristics of primordial chaos, represents the time when things were formless or invisible, dark, void, turbulent, and yet containing the invisible breath of life.

This thought would coincide with Pinch's statement that "the Ogdoad seem to be forces that the creator has to subdue before the work of creation can begin" (176). In those contexts where they are seen as coming together to give life or allow the creator to come into being or make the primordial mound upon which creation can proceed, the primordial mound becomes their tomb. For once the chaos has been subdued, there is room for order to be established.

## Alternative Creator Myths

A possible source of confusion to our western minds is that various texts were written at different times in different locations throughout Egypt, which ascribe the creative act to gods other than Atum or Amun. Naturally, our rational minds want to label such occurrences as contradictory, but there was no sense of contradiction in the minds of the ancient Egyptian people. Whether to say that it was Amun atop the primordial mound who spoke other gods into existence and from there the world, or to ascribe that act to Ra (or Amun-Ra, or Ra-Atum), Shu, Ptah, Khnum, the goddesses

Neith, Hathor or Isis, caused no consternation to them. These were all pathways two some understanding of the invisible, intangible, and perhaps incomprehensible. If the creator god wore another face or was called a different name, the principle was the same. An all-powerful, unknowable reality beyond ourselves was responsible for bringing the world into existence. And this is the truth behind the story.

The primary order of creation from the starting place of the primordial mound was, first, to create the deities who inhabited the invisible divine realm; then, to generate lesser creatures, namely people and animals, to inhabit the world.

The divine separation of Geb and Tefnut, that is, earth and sky, is one of the critical stages in the creative process. The space between them is where humans and animals, and lesser things can live. Likewise, the creation of gender out of an undifferentiated genderless state was essential to the process of creation. Some could be their own fathers or mothers. But in the created realm, it was necessary to establish a duality of male and female. Once the creator god completed that creative act, living beings could procreate and thrive in the home made for them.

That brings us to the third most crucial step in the divine creative process. Having banished chaos and created both divine and mortal creatures, the creator still needed to establish order. This need implies that the absence of disorder does not mean the presence of order. These are intentional, deliberate actions. This principle carried over into the Egyptian worldview, where one must be intentional about not simply avoiding the state of chaos but establishing and preserving order or balance in one's own life and that of others.

## Male and Female: He Created Them

If, as Yuval Harari claims, myths are the fictions we invent and share which become universally believed by groups or even nations, then the story of Atum, Shu, and Tefnut, and the creation of male and female genders deserves to win an award! Imagine for a moment the scene: a boy comes to his mother and father and asks, "Why are boys, boys, and girls, girls?"

Mother replies, "Because that's the way God made us."

"And where did he get that idea? Does God have kids of his own?"

"Well, yes, as a matter of fact, he does."

"And did their mommy push them out of her tummy as you pushed me out?"

"Well, no, not actually...."

"So, where did the kids come from?"

At this point, his mother says, "Go on, Fred, tell your son where God's kids came from?" Mother leaves the room, looking embarrassed. "Well, dad? How did God get kids if they had no mother?"

Now it's father's turn to be embarrassed. "Well, um, you see... It's like this...." *Should I go all in or not,* father asked himself.

"Heck, here goes... You see, son, before he had kids God wasn't a boy or a girl. It was like he was both. But he still had "parts", do you know what I mean?"

The little boy nods, not sure he wants to hear the rest. But there's no stopping now.

Father says, "So, one day he decides he wants children; in fact, he wants twins, a boy, and a girl. But nothing like that has ever been done." Father takes a deep breath. Here it comes. "So, Johnny, he starts touching himself down there, do you understand? He does that until stuff comes out. He puts that into his own mouth and swallows it. And then he coughs or sneezes, or maybe both, and out pops his two kids, Shu, his son, and Tefnut, his daughter."

Johnny's eyes are enormous. Father says, "Do you understand?"

Johnny just turns around and walks away. But the next day at recess, boy, does Johnny have a story to tell!

I can't speak for you, dear reader, but I know I will never forget the story of Shu and Tefnut and their father, Atum! That, my friends, is the incredible power of the story. As Harari points out, it's not only necessary to tell stories but to tell good stories. The difference is that average stories are likely to be dismissed or forgotten and fail to have their desired impact. But, on the other hand, good stories, remembered, retold, and shared from generation to generation, become the myths of our culture, which have the power to shape and define that culture.

We've examined some of the stories of Shu and Tefnut in the previous chapter. They became the first God and Goddess of the pantheon since all other gods before them were not distinguished in gender. When Atum gave them new names and new identities, he introduced foundational concepts into Egyptian thinking. In speaking their new names, he brought the qualities associated with those names into existence. Shu, his son, became Ka, which means "life force or vital essence." Ka became the god who sustains life. Atum's daughter Tefnut became Maat, the principle of truth, justice, and especially order. Maat is the antithesis of *isfet*, chaos. Maat became the favorite daughter of the creator and a source of joy. Maat was the guiding principle of the created world and its people. All Egyptian governors, especially Pharaoh, strove to establish and preserve Maat on earth "as it was in the First Time" (Pinch, 2004, p. 65).

We considered some of the events of this First Time in our brief study of Shu and Tefnut. In Shu's act of separating his children Nut and Geb, the sky and the earth, Shu made life possible and enabled the sun to manifest for the first time as the sun god, Ra. Pinch also mentions that, "as part of establishing the divine order, Shu and Tefnut also become two different types of time. Shu is eternal recurrence, and Tefnut is eternal sameness" (2004, p, 65).

Because of this principle of Maat or eternal sameness, Egyptian civilization hardly changed in over 3000 years. Thus, innovation and change were contrary to the principle of Maat.

## Death and Resurrection

### Osiris and Isis

We come to the most important and foundational story in the canon of Egyptian mythology: the sad and happy tale of Osiris and his sister-mate, Isis. You've met this couple before–the fourth generation of the Ennead of Heliopolis, the children of Geb, lord of the earth, and his sister-mate, Nut, goddess of the sky. The product of their parents' passionate embrace, so close that there was no room between them for creation to occur, yet they could not resist each other's affections. Osiris, the eldest, loves Isis, and she loves him. But their brother Seth is jealous of Osiris. There is murder in his heart. So brutish, reckless Seth devises a plan to take Osiris away from his sister for good. While Osiris sleeps, Seth measures the exact dimensions of his brother's body. Now Osiris must travel into the world for some time to bring agriculture and the domestication of animals to the world as a whole. Seth seizes the opportunity to hatch his plan.

Seth commissions an artisan to craft him a wooden chest, made to his brother's exact shape and dimensions. When Osiris returns home from the world, Seth announces that he will throw a massive banquet in honor of his brother. The evening's entertainment will be a contest, and the prize? A beautiful wooden chest. Each man will have the opportunity to win that prize, and the competition is simple. Each man, in turn, will lay down inside the chest, and the lid will be closed. Whichever man fits perfectly into the chest will get to keep it for himself. Of course, Osiris, the guest of honor, must go first! Seth removes the lid from the chest, and Osiris climbs inside. Seth slams the top down on the chest, seals the chest with molten lead, and throws it into the Nile, where a tributary carries it away from Egypt.

Isis is heartbroken and vows to find her husband and to bring him home for burial. She and her sister Nephthys search across the world, hoping to find their brother. When both are ready to give up the search, Isis finds her lover's wooden chest in Byblos in Lebanon. The wooden chest had washed up onto the shore and grown into a tree, and the owner cut down that tree and made it a pillar in his home. Isis breaks open the box to find her Osiris dead! She and Nephthys bring the body back home and give their brother a proper burial.

Seth is angry that his plans have been thwarted! He digs up the grave, removes his brother, and hacks him into fourteen pieces, which he scatters throughout Egypt. When Isis discovers what her brother Seth has done, she searches through Egypt to gather the pieces together. Isis manages to find thirteen out of fourteen of Osiris' body parts, but his penis is gone, thrown into the Nile, and eaten by fish. Isis, a magician, fashions him another and then, changing into the form of a bird, hovers over him until he comes back to life.

Filled with passion, he impregnates his wife before returning to the underworld to become Lord of the Westerners.

## On Earth, as it is in *A'aru*

Egyptians conceived of their world as containing three realms: *A'aru*, the divine realm in the upper sky described as the Field of Rushes, where its inhabitants would live an idealized version of their earthly farming life; the *Duat*, most often referred to as the Underworld though, in Egyptian thought, it was considered part of the created world and not separate; and the earth, at the center of which stood the nation of Egypt (Pinch, 2004). It appears that the creation of man to inhabit the space between Geb (earth) and Nut (sky) was seen as a more peripheral event than the creation of the Universe, the gods, and pharaoh, a god on earth. His life took on an almost magical significance. By comparison, the average lives of ordinary citizens must have seemed insignificant, except insofar as they participated in and preserved Maat, the divine order. That is not to say that the creator cared nothing for his creation. Coffin

Texts 1130 delineates the "four good deeds" which the creator has performed on behalf of man:

"to create the four winds to give the breath of life to everybody, to make the annual Nile flood so that everyone would get enough food, to create everyone with equal potential, and to make every person's heart remember the West." (Pinch, 2004, p. 67)

It was not until the Middle Kingdom that Egyptians imagined stories to answer how humans came to be. Pinch quotes Coffin Text spell 1130, where the Lord of all claims to have created deities from his sweat and "people from the tears of my eye" (2004, p. 66). It is uncertain how much weight to give to the observation, but the ancient Egyptian words for "tears" and "people" sound almost identical. Perhaps the history of Egypt and, by extension, of the world bears out that exciting parallelism.

We observed in the previous chapter that Egyptians recognized the gods Khnum and Ptah as those who crafted the bodies of the gods and people, the former out of precious materials and the latter out of mud or clay. Khnum is depicted as using a potter's wheel to fashion the creatures of the earth. Khnum would, in fact, fashion two bodies for each individual: one body before birth and a second to house an individual's vital essence, or Ka.

## To *Duat,* the Underworld

Duat is many things in Egyptian mythology, but the most evocative word to our western minds is Underworld–not to be confused with the Judeo-Christian concept of Hell or Hades since the Hebrew and Greek scriptures which reference these concepts would not be written for more than two millennia. Nor should we think of Duat as being somehow removed from creation, like an alternate but invisible dimension. On the contrary, the ancient Egyptians believed that Duat was the lowermost of three realms of creation, the other two being the earth and the upper sky. Duat, therefore, was still part of the world, nearer than we might conceive. It was believed to be the realm of the dead and the residence, in fact, of several gods, the most important by far in Egyptian belief being Osiris, Lord of the Underworld. Osiris was the pattern for all to follow. He was the first mummy and the first to be reborn from his mummified condition as a reward for having passed the weighing of the heart, the final ritual of the judgment of one's life.

Duat represented the journey of the soul of the deceased through various ordeals on its way to final judgment and the prospect of an afterlife in A'aru. Osiris and different resident gods appeared to the departed soul, often accompanying it on portions of its journey. Sometimes grotesque, demon-like figures appeared, trying the soul on its journey. The deceased had to face a tribunal of 42 judges, each of whom evaluated a different aspect of the soul's spiritual fitness to continue the journey. The dead must persuade each of the judges, in turn, that he is innocent of a total of 42 specific sins or that circumstances should enable him to be excused if he has committed any. If successful in his persuasion of the judges and the passing of the many ordeals and challenges, he would stand before Anubis, who would weigh his heart against the feather of Maat, standing for truth and justice. If the soul's heart were heavier than the feather, it was rejected and then consumed by Ammit, the devourer of souls. There was no hell in the Egyptian worldview–the deceased, in this case, was denied an afterlife altogether and ceased to exist.

Duat was not merely the setting for the journey of deceased souls on their way to judgment and either life in A'aru or extermination. Divided into twelve sections, it represented the twelve hours of the night through which the sun god, Ra, traveled from sunset (west) to sunrise (east). From the vantage point of Atet, the solar barge which floated on the Primordial Waters, Ra passed through the hours of the night, shining his rays on the souls of the deceased who slept and reviving them for that one hour. At the same time, throughout the night, Ra fought to defeat Apep or Apophis, the serpent who represented chaos, so that the sun–himself–would rise the following day. At his rising, Ra manifested himself as the youthful god of sunrise, Khepri, while at sunset, he embodied the aged creator god Atum. Between these two points, he was Ra, god of the noonday sun.

# Chapter 5: The Drama Unfolds

In chapters 1-3, we have explored ancient Egyptian society from the outside looking in. In our mind's eye, we have glimpsed the world of Egypt as it might have been. Our vision may correspond at least in part to the reality of that old place and time. But this reality is more like an enormous jigsaw puzzle, complete at the edges but missing many of its connecting pieces and without the benefit of the box lid. We study the pieces we have, wanting to see the whole picture. Nonetheless, we recognize that "evidence for lives and events so distant from our own time will, regrettably, forever remain incomplete" (Shaw, 2014), and so will be our understanding. Yet the lure of the mysterious and the unknown continues to hold us in its grip.

Our first glimpse of that far-away culture has been from the bank of the Nile, which defines the country and its people. In that river, we discover a connection with the past. The eternal Nile remains, despite the onrush of modern civilization, while the former glories of Egypt are in ruins. The river itself fuels our imagination. From that vantage point of creativity, we have imagined the rich black soil of *iteru* between our bare toes and strained our ears to hear the first rush of water as the inundation arrives in the summer season. We have stopped for a moment to witness the everyday activities of freemen, slaves, and serfs in their kilts who work the fertile alluvial soil–the gift of Hapy, the god of the inundation–as *iteru* recedes, planting crops of barley and wheat, or graze their flocks of sheep and goats and pasture their cattle on the narrow, flat floodplain.

We have listened to the gaggle of commerce as government businessmen trade stories and haggle the price of goods with swarthy traders from across the Red Land or as lone hawkers barter the surplus goods of their estate masters. We have seen scribes in their long skirts, carrying wooden palettes with writing brushes and ink pots, returning to their homes from work in government positions or as clerks or accountants. We have remarked on the distinctive appearance of the Wab priests, hairless, clothed in their linen robes and papyrus sandals, approaching the entrance to their temples in service of local or national deities. We have caught the measured, almost rhythmic, sound of artisans transforming gold, silver, and copper, turquoise and lapis lazuli into breathtaking designs for wealthy patrons or the royal court, or else shaping wood, stone or bronze with rudimentary tools into the forms of animals, persons, even gods; witnessed the dangerous and backbreaking efforts of miners, mining treasures they will never possess, and quarrymen cutting massive blocks of limestone (or sandstone during the New Kingdom) with astounding precision for tombs, temples, and pyramids; and listened to the gentle lapping of the waters of Mehit, the Delta, against the sides of marshmen's punts as they weave through papyrus stands with their knives ready to harvest one of Egypt's most significant natural commodities.

We have encountered Pharaoh–not yet the individual men and women who rose to absolute power throughout successive dynasties, first as incarnations of Horus and later as sons and daughters of Ra but, instead, the idea of Pharaoh as the lead actor in a massive spectacle, whose primary role evolved through the Predynastic era (before 3150 BCE) and was first realized in the person and reign of Narmur at the beginning of Egyptian history. Finally, we have glimpsed Pharaoh at the pinnacle of an enormous civil and religious structure that promised order and prevented chaos, like the gods themselves in primordial times.

We have been introduced to many gods and goddesses who were believed to inhabit the invisible world and manifest their power and presence in our own. And in listening to the stories of their actions and their exploits, and of the beliefs which shaped the human journey from birth to death and beyond, we have drawn a little closer to understanding the worldview of the People of the Black Land.

## The Outline

Now, imagine yourself a famous director. Your producer has just spun out to you her idea for a stage play–not some one-night-only, off-Broadway kind of production. This idea has epic written prominently on every page. Egypt. Ancient Egypt. You've spent several cups of coffee listening as she unravels the backstory: the Nile at the inundation, kingdoms at war, victory and unification, prosperity, pharaohs, and priests, gods and goddesses, myths and magic, death, the Underworld, rebirth. Her hands are waving in the air. You know she's excited about the whole thing. Frankly, so are you.

"Pyramids?"

"Yep, she says."

"And mummies?"

"It wouldn't be Egypt without mummies," she says, leaning in. You're hooked, and she knows it. Reaching into her bag, she produces a document, not thick but well-worn, with a single staple, upper left corner. You recognize it: a planning outline for a three-act play (much like you see below). It's not the script–too soon for that. This will give you an idea of the flow, she says, the main characters, the highlights. Standing up, she pushes the outline across the table.

"Read it," she says. And she walks away.

You reach for the manuscript, fold the dog-eared corner to page one, and begin to read...Narmer, the first king of unified Egypt....Your imagination soars. The stage is set. In your mind's eye, the characters assume their roles and take their positions. The curtain is ready to come up on the first act in Egyptian civilization's grand historical drama.

Cue the lights, you whisper, and...action!

## Cast of Characters

### The Early Kingdom Period

**Narmer** (c. 3150 BCE): he ruled during the Naqada III period in Upper Egypt. He conquered

Lower Egypt c. 3150 BCE to establish the First Dynasty of a unified ancient Egypt. Narmer led from Thinis.

**Khasekhemwy** (c.2704-2686 BCE): last ruler of the Second Dynasty, an obscure period in Egyptian history. Khasekhemwy ruled from Thinis. He is believed to have been the father of **Djoser** (see below).

**Djoser** (c. 2686-2668 BCE): first ruler of the Third Dynasty. Djoser may have been responsible for moving the capital of Egypt from Thinis to **Memphis.** In addition, he designed step pyramids at Saqqara, where he was buried.

**Sneferu** (c. 2613-2589 BCE): first ruler of the Fourth Dynasty. He experimented with step pyramid design, ultimately building the first true smooth-sided pyramid.

**Khufu** (c. 2589-2566 BCE): second ruler of the Fourth Dynasty. He built the Great Pyramid at Giza, the last remaining of the Seven Wonders of the Ancient World, over 20 years.

**Khafre** (c. 2558-2532 BCE): the fourth ruler of the Fourth Dynasty, and son of **Khufu,** built the third of three pyramids on the Giza plateau, beside the Great Pyramid.

**Unas** (c. 2375-2345 BCE): believed to be the last ruler of the Fifth Dynasty. He built a smaller pyramid at Saqqara, the burial chamber boasting the first hieroglyphic inscriptions of any pyramid, the Pyramid Texts.

**Pepi II** (c. 2278-2184 BCE): second last ruler of the Sixth Dynasty and the Early Kingdom altogether, he ruled for 94 years. During his reign, pharaonic power crumbled, leading to the First Intermediate Period within three years of his death (c. 2181-2041).

**The Middle Kingdom Period**

**Mentuhotep II** (c. 2060-2010 BCE): sixth ruler of the Eleventh Dynasty, put down an insurrection at Abydos, reuniting Upper and Lower Egypt to end the First Intermediate Period to the Middle Kingdom. Mentuhotep II ruled from Thebes.

**Amenemhat I** (c. 1991-1962 BCE): first ruler of the Twelfth Dynasty. He worshipped the local deity of Thebes, Amun, the creator god, and the

"Hidden One," who would become the principal deity of Egypt. He ruled from It-towe, 10 miles south of Memphis.

## The New Kingdom Period

**Ahmose** (c. 1570-1546 BCE): the first ruler of the Eighteenth Dynasty and the New Kingdom period, he crushed both Hyksos and Kushite kingdoms, reunifying Egypt. He ruled from Thebes.

**Tuthmosis I** (c. 1524-1518 BCE): third ruler of the Eighteenth Dynasty. Tuthmosis I was a commoner who married the eldest royal princess to obtain the throne. He was known for his extensive military conquests and establishing the Valley of the Kings for his own and successive underground burials. Tuthmosis I ruled from Thebes.

**Hatshepsut** (c. 1498-1483 BCE): the "Foremost of Noble Ladies," as her name is translated, was one of four children of Pharaoh Tuthmosis I and grew up in the royal household. While she was still a child, her two brothers and sister died, making her an only child. Her father, wishing to secure the dynasty for his own family before he died, married Hatshepsut to a half-brother who later became Tuthmosis II. Her husband was sickly, however, and died without an heir. As a result, Hatshepsut seized the role of regent when the 10-year-old son of a lesser wife was crowned pharaoh **Tuthmosis III** (see below). Two years later, Hatshepsut took for herself the title of Pharaoh and reigned for 22 years until her death. She chose to dress like a pharaoh, and she even wore the ceremonial beard and short kilt of her male counterparts. Moreover, she claimed to be the daughter of the ancient creator god Amun.

**Tuthmosis III** (c.1504-1430 BCE): the sixth ruler of the Eighteenth Dynasty, he distinguished himself through extensive military campaigns over his 54-year reign. His father died when Tuthmosis III was only two or three years old, yet he was officially crowned Pharaoh. His aunt, Hatshepsut, assumed the role of regent and, within two years, took for herself the title of Pharaoh. When Hatshepsut died after 22 years, Tuthmosis II ascended the throne. He is distinguished for his military prowess and for leading more than 17 campaigns. He conquered hundreds of cities and expanded the Egyptian

Empire to include Nubia in the far south and Canaan and southern Syria in the Levant.

**Amenhotep IV/Akhenaten** (c. 1350-1334 BCE): the eleventh ruler of the Eighteenth Dynasty, attempted to replace the ancient Egyptian religion with the monotheistic worship of *Aten*, the visible orb of the sun. He ruled from Akhetaten, near modern-day Tel Amarna.

**Ramesses II** (c. 1279-1212 BCE): called "The Great." He was the second son of Pharaoh Seti I and a member of the royal household, though his older brother was next-in-line to the throne. Unfortunately, that brother died when Ramesses II was 14 years old so that Ramesses II became the Prince of Egypt. He took for himself two wives, Nefertari and Isetnofret. Nefertari became Ramessses' chief wife when he ascended the throne of Egypt at 25 years of age, upon the death of his father Seti I, and Nefertari ruled beside him during his 66-year reign. Ramesses II was the third ruler of the Nineteenth Dynasty of the New Kingdom Period.

After the expulsion of the Hyksos from the northern Delta where they had established a stronghold during the Second Intermediate

Period, the pharaohs recognized the critical need to establish buffer zones at their borders to prevent future invasion. Ramesses II eagerly pressed this agenda with a series of aggressive military campaigns against Nubians to the south, Libyans across the Red Land, and Syrians and Hittites northward in the Levant. He led the 20,000-strong Egyptian army, equipped with some 5,000 chariots, against a Hittite force more than twice as strong at the Battle of Kadesh, the oldest recorded battle in history. The battle ended with a stalemate, and later a peace treaty, with the Hittite nation which lasted for the duration of Ramesses II's reign.

Ramesses II distinguished himself as a great warrior and military leader. His military achievements were chiseled into stone from one end of the Nile Valley to the other. Ramesses II was also known for having the names and glyphs of former pharaohs removed from records of their achievements and replaced with his own! Moreover, Ramesses II was responsible for a multitude of building projects featuring his own likeness, including the giant statue at his Mortuary Temple on the west bank of the Nile near Thebes, and a series of four giant, seated statues of Ramesses II which adorn the temple facade of Abu Simbel. Ramesses II also built a new capital city which was used during his reign but was later abandoned: Pi-Ramesses. Pharaoh Ramesses II died at around 90 years of age, and was initially buried on the western bank of the river, in the Valley of the Kings. His mummy was later moved to protect it from tomb robbers. The mummy of Ramesses II the Great now resides in the Grand Egyptian Museum at Giza, just outside Cairo.

**Ramesses III** (c. 1182-1151 BCE): second ruler of the Twentieth Dynasty, led a mighty land and sea battle in the Delta, turning away invading tribes to save Egypt. He built a great temple on the west bank of the Nile opposite Thebes. His reign was marked by a gradual decline, leading to the Late Period (c. 1070-332 BCE).

**The Ptolemaic Period**

**Alexander the Great** (c. 332-323 BCE): As Alexander the Great expanded his empire throughout Europe, Asia, and the territories of the Persian Empire, he took control of Egypt by sheer military might. From Egypt, Alexander sought to expand his Empire eastward, towards the Indus Valley. Alexander was eventually undermined by his own troops, who desired to return to Greece. He died of fever during the return journey at the age of 33.

**Ptolemy I Soter I** (c. 304-284 BCE): first ruler of the Thirty-second, and last, Dynasty. He had commanded Alexander the Great's personal guard, until the latter died in 332 BCE. After nine years of ensuing turmoil, Ptolemy seized control of Egypt, founding an all-Greek dynasty which endured until its thirteenth ruler, **Cleopatra VII** (see below), committed suicide, bringing ancient Egypt's independent history to an end.

**Cleopatra VII** (51-30 BCE): the last pharaoh of the Thirty-second, or Ptolemaic, Dynasty and of ancient Egypt itself, and the favorite daughter of Pharaoh Ptolemy XII, Cleopatra VII grew up in the royal household with all its privileges, including education. She could speak, read, and write Greek since her father and the entire Ptolemaic Dynasty before him were of Greek descent. But her education included at least six other languages, including Egyptian and Latin. She was intelligent, capable and ambitious for herself and for her son, Caesarion, whose father was Julius Caesar.

## Prologue

**Setting**: the ancient city of **Thinis**, believed to have been located near Abydos. Thinis had been the center of a confederacy of tribes in Upper Egypt until its leader, Narmer, conquered Lower Egypt and united the Two Lands. Thinis then became the capital city of unified Egypt.

**Time:** The Early Dynastic Era (3150-2686 BCE)

**Synopsis:** The earliest known example of a story utilizing the Egyptian writing system we know as hieroglyphics is called the Narmer Palette, after Narmer (believed to be the same person as *Menes*), the ruler of Upper Egypt who conquered Lower Egypt to unite the Two Lands under one government. A six-inch stone palette was commonly used in early Egyptian culture to mix cosmetic eye shadow. This palette, however, was two feet tall, carved on both sides with rudimentary writing and bas-relief sculpture, and was intended to tell a story: the story of Narmer's victory and the establishment thereby of the First Dynasty of a centralized Egyptian government. Incidentally, this palette marks the beginning of Egyptian history. It is ground zero for the civilization which spanned 31 centuries!

Not much more is known for sure of Narmer, though other archaeological finds corroborate the evidence of the Narmer Palette. Narmer was believed to be the ruler of a southern tribal confederacy. One side of the palette shows Narmer wearing the "White Crown of the South" and "leading a procession of tiny figures carrying banners" (Brier & Hoyt Hobbs, 2013, p. 11) which are believed to represent the various tribal allies. The reverse of the Palette displays Narmer wearing the Red Crown of the North and wielding a mace to strike down his enemy. Archaeologists found the macehead depicted on the palette in the same dig as the palette itself, which, moreover, is inscribed with the name Narmer.

Narmer consolidated power to found the First Dynasty of Egyptian civilization. Relatively little is known of his successors, whose reign spanned the First and Second Dynasties of the Early Dynastic Period. There seems little overt significance to their individual accomplishments until the rule of Khasekhemwy, the last ruler of the Second Dynasty and of the Early Dynastic period itself. He is credited with restoring order and unity to Egypt after a period of unrest, possibly civil war, between rival devotees of the Horus and Set cults. His royal glyph or insignia, unique in Egyptian history, includes the symbols for both names.

Khasekhemwy also initiated several building projects during his reign, the most significant of which is a vast mud-brick enclosure called Shunet El Zebib, or "raisin barn" in Arabic, built at Abydos c. 2700 BCE. Its original purpose is unknown, but details of its structure evoke the later step pyramids built by Khasekhemwy's son, Djoser. In light of these similarities and of the imminent boom in the building of royal tombs and mortuary temples, beginning in earnest with Djoser's step pyramids, we may safely infer that Egyptians were thinking more deeply, and asking themselves more pointed questions, about death, the Afterlife, and what ought to be done by the living to prepare for these. By the living we mean, of course, the pharaohs, since the Egyptian cosmos afforded little room for consideration of the plight of average mortals. It turns out that the Third and Fourth Dynasties would supply concrete answers to such questions.

## Act I

**Setting:** Memphis, a city at the mouth of the Nile Delta 12 miles south of Giza in Lower Egypt. Its origin predates the unification of Egypt, and legend ascribes its foundation to Menes/Narmer. Memphis became the capital of Egypt around the beginning of the Third Dynasty.

**Time:** the Old Kingdom Era (2686-2181 BCE)

**Synopsis:** This period is rightly called The Age of the Pyramids, though Djoser deserves credit for the original thought which precipitated the building frenzy. The idea of containing a sand-pit burial within a sloped, rectangular enclosure, called a *mastaba*, was not new (see chapter 7). Enclosing several elaborate burial and storage chambers inside a mastaba 397 ft. x 358 ft. sq at the base, rising in six layers like "a 200-foot-high facsimile of a wedding cake" (Brier & Hoyt Hobbs, 2013, p.179), was novel. The architectural genius who designed this remarkable structure was Imhotep, chancellor to Pharaoh Djoser and high priest of Ra, who later in Egyptian history was given the status of a god. Imhotep's forward-thinking and design failed to prevent robbers from emptying the tomb, however.

Snefru, the first pharaoh of the Fourth Dynasty, set out to improve upon the innovative step pyramid of his predecessor in designing his tomb. We would recognize his concept as a true pyramid in design. Unlike that of his successor Khufu, Snefru's pyramids—he constructed three in total—were simply modified step pyramids. He filled in the steps of successive courses with dressed stone to render the smooth-sided appearance we recognize today. Snefru could not finish his first attempt because its sides were too steep and unstable for its soft limestone casing. The second, or bent, pyramid started too steep, and its builders had to use a more shallow wall angle from the halfway point to prevent its collapse. The third and final attempt was a success: That same shallow slope angle and broader base ensured that the pyramid would stand the test of time. It still stands today, at Saqqara, as the earliest extant example of a true pyramid.

The history of the Fourth Dynasty reached its zenith with the construction of what became known as the Great Pyramid of Khufu, Snefru's son, on the Giza plateau a short distance from the capital, Memphis (see chapter 7). There had been pyramids of various kinds before, as there would be after (Khufu's son, Khafra, for example, would build a pyramid almost as glorious as that of his father, beside the Great Pyramid; it is recognizable for the iconic 200-foot long Sphinx guarding the tomb). But Khufu's tomb stands alone. It was the tallest free-standing structure on earth for almost four millennia. And, once considered one of the Seven Wonders of the Ancient World, it remains a Wonder to this day. To think of Egypt is to think of the pyramids, and in particular of the Great Pyramid. What was once designed as the "resurrection machine" of Pharaoh Khufu has become the singular memorial of a great ancient culture.

The long reign of Pepi II (c. 2278-2184 BCE), the second-to-last ruler of the Old Kingdom, coincided with the gradual breakdown of stable, centralized political authority. Bureaucrats sought to entrench themselves and their families in positions of power, often away from the national capital. Nomarchs vied for control of their own and other nomes throughout Upper and Lower Egypt. The leadership base of the country was fragmented. Some might be tempted to blame Pepi II for what they assume was weak and ineffectual rule, as though he allowed things to get out of control. And yet the longevity of a 94-year rule–perhaps the longest reign of any pharaoh in Egyptian history–should be the hallmark of stable government. What other factor might have contributed to Egypt's drifting into the period of anarchy following the death of Pepi II? Cox holds the key to this mystery: "The annual flooding of the Nile...provided the framework by which the society was held together" (Harvey Gallagher Cox, 2013, p. 27). Barbara Bell has described how the level of the annual Nile inundation began to drop by the end of the First Dynasty, and continued to fall throughout the Second to at least the Fifth, according to the oldest existing records (Bell, 1970). By the reign of Pharaoh Sahure (c. 2490 BCE), the inundation had risen only 2.48 cubits, or 4.33 feet (Bell, 1970). Remember that, according to the Roman historian Pliny, "in a rise of twelve cubits, [Egypt] senses famine" (Wilkinson, Toby, 2015). Many historians agree that progressively lower annual inundations over several centuries of the Early Kingdom, up to and including the reign of Pepi II, must have precipitated serious famine and the subsequent collapse of the "framework by which the society was held together" (Cox, 2013, p. 27).

## First Intermission

## First Intermediate Period (2181-2040 BCE)

This 141-year period in ancient Egyptian history, sandwiched between the glories of the Old Kingdom–the unification of Upper and Lower Kingdoms under Narmur, and the construction of numerous pyramids both at Saqqara and on the Giza plateau–and the restoration of political and civil order under the Mentuhotep, Amenemhat, and Senusret pharaohs during the Middle Kingdom, epitomizes the chaos which was so repugnant to the Egyptian psyche. According to Manetho, the 3rd century BCE priest mentioned earlier who introduced the concept of dynasties to lend structure to the span of Egyptian history, no less than 140 individuals laid claim to the title of pharaoh during this time of weakened royal authority, political maneuvering, and civil war. Since it seems unlikely, if not impossible, that the country had a new pharaoh every year over several average Egyptian lifetimes, we can safely infer that more than a few of these "ephemeral kings" (Wilkinson, 2013) ruled simultaneously and from different capitals. Manetho identified at least three different dynasties in his reckoning of this turbulent and uncertain time.

With the absolute rule of the pharaohs weakened and diluted in this way, government and civil administrators seized the opportunity afforded by the resulting power vacuum to expand their influence significantly and to secure their own and their families' futures. Appointed positions gradually became hereditary possessions without a stable, higher authority to provide necessary checks and balances. Furthermore, Egyptian infrastructure and economy were driven, as we saw in chapters two and three, by the ability of the pharaoh, the Son of Ra and the incarnation of Horus, to mobilize the entire population of Egypt in unquestioning obedience to his divine will and with promises of favorable treatment in the next life, where he would once again be their pharaoh. In the absence of that one clear voice of command and comfort, the building of monuments, tombs, and temples all but ceased.

This unfortunate episode in the history of Egyptian civilization deserves the epithet Dark Age. Brier and Hobbs reference the following excerpt from a papyrus written by some unnamed eyewitness to the crisis which characterized this period, as follows:

The bowman is ready. The wrongdoer is everywhere. There is no man of yesterday. A man goes out to plow with his shield. A man smites his brother, his mother's son. Men sit in the bushes until the benighted traveler comes in order to plunder his load. The robber is the possessor of riches. Boxes of ebony are broken up. Precious acacia wood is cleft asunder. (Brier & A Hoyt Hobbs, 2013, p. 20).

We can hardly appreciate to what extent the inner turmoil of gods-fearing Egyptian citizens might have mirrored that without, given what we know of their worldview, unless we attempt to reach across the millennia with the eyes of our imagination. Yet can we not hear a faint echo from this turbulent past in the midst of the noise of our today? It reminds us that the drama of these people, upon whose lives the curtain has long ago fallen, is not merely an ancient Egyptian drama—it is a *human* drama, after all. And as with any drama, it is just at that point when all hope seems lost, that we eagerly await a hero who will set things right.

## Act II

**Setting:** Thebes, capital city during the Eleventh Dynasty; and It-towe, ten miles south of Memphis, which became the new capital city of Egypt under the reign of Amenemhet I, at the beginning of the Twelfth Dynasty.

**Time:** The Middle Kingdom Era (2060-1782 BCE)

**Synopsis:** The Egyptian people found their hero in Mentuhotep II (2060-2010 BCE). Previous rulers, all bearing the name Intef, had tried unsuccessfully to restore Maat, order, to the Two Lands. What the country needed was not a diplomat or a politician, but a strong warrior, someone with whom the war god ("Mentu") is pleased ("hotep"). Mentuhotep II took for his Horus name the descriptor, "He Gives Life to the Heart of the Two Lands," and, later, "Uniter of the Two Lands." Historians point out that his statues display his "brute power" but are "crude and poorly worked" (Brier, 1999), suggesting that the artistry and craftsmanship of the Early Kingdom were lost during the time of chaos. What may also have been lost, for the time being, is that belief in pharaohs who depicted themselves as immortal and above the rest of humanity. 141 years of very human struggle led the Egyptian people to appreciate real men of bone and sinew, men who could fight and bleed for the sake of reunifying their country. The records of Mentuhotep's valiant efforts are scattered up and down the Nile. His sons who succeeded him were likewise men of action, undertaking great expeditions for the sake of rebuilding their country

Amenemhet I (c 1991-1962 BCE), the first ruler of the Twelfth Dynasty, was "a commoner who did great things" (Brier, 1999, p. 38), including establishing a new capital, It-towe or Binder of Two Lands, strategically placed in the Faiyum instead of at Memphis or Thebes. His successors took measures to increase agricultural production there, including the building of a 30-mile long canal to bring the Nile's water to the Faiyum. Amenemhet I's reign inaugurated what is considered to be the Golden Age of the Middle Kingdom Period; it was a time of stability and expansion, particularly south into Kush (as far as the Second and Third Cataract) and north into southern Canaan in the Levant.

During this amazing period of Egyptian history, art evolved in elegantly realistic directions, some of the most refined literature in the Egyptian language was produced, and building projects displayed a level of skill and refinement that still speaks for them to this day.

# Second Intermission

### Second Intermediate Period (1782-1570 BCE)

Have you heard the familiar refrain: second verse, same as the first? That describes perfectly this second period of chaos and turmoil in ancient Egypt. The quelling of civil war and the social upheaval which followed in its wake by Mentuhotep II, which inaugurated the Middle Kingdom period, must have offered Egyptian citizens a renewed sense of hope for the rebirth of their nation after the disastrous events of the previous 140 years. Whole generations had passed into Duat, the Farworld of departed souls seeking passage to the Field of Reeds, while their familiar and comforting social and political order had crumbled. They had needed some strong deliverer to re-establish that order, and Mentuhotep II had accomplished that heavy task.

Now, 400 years later, the Egyptian people found themselves in a similar, yet at once even worse, situation than before. Over more than 200 years, Egyptian rule once again became fragmented, with more than 160 individuals from three dynasties vying for the pharaonic throne. Weakened from within, they found themselves beset by powerful foreign invaders who had emigrated from the Levant and established a power base in the far northeast of Lower Egypt at Avaris. These infiltrators, Indo-Europeans who called themselves Hyksos, adopted many of the features and practices of Egyptian culture. Yet, they did not fool the proud and insular Egyptian people: to the Egyptian, these immigrants were despicable foreigners. They should be driven out of the country. That task would fall to the rulers of what became the 17th dynasty and, ultimately, to the pharaoh Ahmose, the first king of the 18th dynasty, whose victories opened the door to the glories of the 500-year New Kingdom (1570-1070 BCE).

## Act III

**Setting:** Thebes, during the Seventeenth Dynasty; the first of the Eighteenth Dynasty until the succession of Akhenaten; the rest of the Eighteenth Dynasty after Akhenaten, and the first portion of the Nineteenth Dynasty until the succession of Rameses II the Great; Akhetaten, the new capital city under the reign of Akhenaten; Pi-Ramses during the reign of Rameses II in the Nineteenth Dynasty; and Memphis, following the death of Rameses II and throughout the Twentieth Dynasty.

**Time:** the New Kingdom Era (1570-1070 BCE)

**Synopsis:** The New Kingdom witnessed the transformation of Egypt from an isolated country to a vast empire, through the military conquests and political alliances forged by a series of powerful and dynamic leaders. Increased wealth spurred grand building projects, including the Temple of Luxor at Thebes and major expansion of the Temple of Karnak. Ramesses II chiseled his name and accomplishments over much of Egypt, and erected massive monuments to himself, including the Temple of Abu Simbel, which boasts four massive seated statues of the pharaoh across its facade. Hatshepsut built a spectacular Mortuary Temple carved into the base of a mountain. The pharaohs of the Eighteenth, Nineteenth and Twentieth Dynasties wanted to be sure that their names and deeds would never be forgotten. It seems they achieved that desire. And the Valley of the Kings, for 500 years the burial ground of New Kingdom pharaohs, has yielded up unimaginable treasures in the early 20th century which would forever secure its place as among the most iconic and memorable features of ancient Egypt.

# Epilogue

## The Late Period (1070-332 BCE)

This was a time of decline, from the glorious days of the New Kingdom Period, during which other nations occupied Egypt and brought with them foreign speech, different customs, and the gradual dilution and disintegration of indigenous Egyptian culture. This and the Ptolemaic Period which followed are absent from the chronologies of some historians, who feel that the true Egypt perished with the invasions of Nubian, Libyan, Kushite, Persian and Greek peoples over more than 700 years. However, the role of Pharaoh did not disappear from history until the death of its last representative, Cleopatra VII.

## The Ptolemaic Period (323-30 BCE)

The Ptolemaic Dynasty had ruled ancient Egypt for more than 250 years when Cleopatra VII was born. Cleopatra's father died when she was 18 years old, having left the throne to her and Ptolemy XIII, her 10-year-old brother. The two married and together assumed the throne of Egypt; but, given their age difference, Cleopatra could assert more authority than her brother, becoming the de facto Pharaoh. The younger Ptolemy was not pleased with his sister's apparent usurping of authority. When he was 13 years old, Ptolemy expelled Cleopatra from the palace and assumed the throne as Pharaoh.

Julius Caesar arrived in Egypt in 48 BC, and Ptolemy XIII welcomed him to the palace. While Caesar was there, Cleopatra allegedly snuck back into the palace inside a rolled-up carpet and enlisted his aid to overthrow her brother. Caesar defeated the Egyptian army at the Battle of the Nile, and Ptolemy XIII drowned in the river while attempting to escape. Cleopatra once more took the throne as Pharaoh, co-ruling with another brother, Ptolemy XIV. Cleopatra VII strengthened the Egyptian economy, establishing lucrative trade relations with surrounding nations and increasing Egypt's prosperity, which contributed to her popularity with the Egyptian people. Despite her relationship with Caesar, and notwithstanding that she was Greek, and the descendant of Greeks as far back as the days of Alexander the Great, Cleopatra VII may have considered herself Egyptian, and wanted to preserve her country's independence.

Cleopatra and Julius Caesar became lovers, and he fathered a son by her, named Caesarion. This son would eventually become the last king of Egypt, co-ruling with his mother. Cleopatra had visited Rome and was staying in one of Caesar's country houses when he was assassinated on March 15, 44 BCE. Cleopatra returned thereafter to Egypt where, in 41 BCE, she met Mark Antony, one of the Roman leaders who were vying for power after Caesar's murder. Cleopatra fell in love with Mark Antony and enlisted his support against Caesar's legitimate heir, Octavian, desiring instead to put her own son Caesarion on the throne of the Roman Empire. Mark Antony had declared Caesarion to be Caesar's legal heir, pitting himself against Octavian in a contest for control of the Roman Empire.

The combined armies of Cleopatra and Mark Antony clashed with Octavian's forces at the Battle of Actium. The two were defeated and fled to Egypt. Antony made another attempt to defeat Octavian, but realized that he would once again be defeated and taken prisoner by Octavian's superior forces. In the midst of battle, Antony heard the false report that Cleopatra was dead, and took his own life. When Cleopatra heard that Antony was dead, she committed suicide, possibly by self-administering some kind of poison or by exposing herself to the bite of a venomous snake. Later that year, Caesarion, the son of Cleopatra VII and Julius Caesar, was murdered. Ancient Egypt was dead, absorbed into the Roman Empire of Octavian who took the name Augustus as the first Emperor of Rome.

# Chapter 6: Pit Graves to Pyramids

## It's the *Pits,* Man!

We've witnessed the development of an Egyptian worldview centered upon the Afterlife, particularly upon resurrection–the reanimation of the deceased person, the reunion of his body with *Ba*, the soul, and *Ka*, the vital essence, and the prospect of eternal life within that body. I'm convinced that the germ of this worldview came from at least as far back in time as the Predynastic period and the resettlement of modern humans in the Nile Valley eleven millennia ago. Do you remember the most basic form of burial discovered by archaeologists throughout the Valley? Think of its elements: a body placed into a shallow sandpit; legs contracted into a fetal position; the body laying on its left side, its head pointing south so that the body faces to the west. At first, the body is simply covered with warm sand. Later, we see the body covered by an animal hide, perhaps laying on a reed mat. Later still, we see a young woman in that same kind of sandpit, in the same position, but now she's wrapped in linen cloth and fur. Instead of a solitary grave, there are cemeteries. Graves become more ornate, and offerings of food, clothing, and other personal effects are placed within. Some of the deceased were wealthy: their tombs are larger still, more elaborate, while the graves of the poor are more humble.

Egyptian prehistory has supplied us with ample clues regarding the *why* of these aspects of death and burial, which shine a light on the embryonic worldview of Egypt. The bodies of loved ones (not enemies–these were dumped, unceremoniously, in mass graves) needed to be positioned carefully to face the west. Why? The more fully-developed worldview of later centuries suggests that the west was the source of rebirth or reincarnation. The disposition of the dead body was somehow connected to the disposition of the soul. The evolution of preservative techniques confirms this thinking that the physical body was essential to the Afterlife experience. Bodies needed to remain intact (a nod here to the Osiris-Isis myth and the consequent need for Isis to fashion an artificial phallus for her husband) while that which animated them was on the other side. Natural mummification by sand-pit burial progressed to the wrapping of the body with furs and, later, with strips of linen. Yet, the Egyptians could still not prevent the process of decay. At some point, they must have made the connection between the presence of the soft organs and the decomposition process (remember, the Egyptians had no science–only best guesses). The answer? Remove the soft organs before burial. Then, too, if sand possessed some preservative properties, salt would be far better! Enter natron, a salt combination found in only one place in the world–Egypt! Remove the internal organs, bury the body in natron for a lengthy period, remove the desiccated body and clean it, and then–that's right, wrap it in strips of linen! There we have the deliberate mummification process, a logical outcome of the developing Egyptian worldview. We'll look more closely at the details in the next chapter. For now, let's consider the development of what we might consider the "mummy house."

Sandpits have been topped with one mastaba, then another, and another. So there you have, the step pyramid of Djoser! Nice, but we can do better! What if we were to make it bigger, taller, and smooth out the sides? Why, of course, then you'd have...

## The Great Pyramid of Khufu

It's not customary to tell a story by starting at the end. Nonetheless, we need to keep the following nutshell summary at the forefront of our thinking as we approach the question: How on earth did they do that?

The statistics associated with the great pyramid of Khufu are humbling: 2,300,000 blocks of stone, each weighing an average of 2 tons, set in place at a rate of one block every two minutes for 10 hours a day over a period of at least 20 years; alignment to true north with an error of only one-twentieth of a degree; and a finished height of 481 feet, making it the tallest building in the world until the construction of the great European cathedrals (Wilkinson, Toby, 2015).

That's the end of the story! But let's travel in our imaginations to the other end, that is, to the beginning of the project – indeed, before the project began. Imagine that you are the king's nephew, Hemiunu and that you've been commissioned to oversee what by rights is the grandest and most ambitious construction project known to man. After consulting the gods and collaborating with the royal engineers, you've selected a site atop the rugged limestone plateau of Giza, within spitting distance of the great monuments of previous dynasties at Saqqara. From where you stand, you can see the pyramids in the distance. An impressive effort, no doubt, but the scale of this undertaking will leave them all behind. And so, there you stand on that limestone plateau as the sun is setting. And you begin to see the faint twinkle of the Polar Star. This will be the destination of your resurrected pharaoh. But so that he does not lose his way after that resurrection, he looks to the structure to orient him in space. Your pyramid must be ideally situated and precisely aligned with the North star. There can be no room for error. The afterlife of your pharaoh depends upon it. Perhaps, your own life depends upon it as well. But how to be sure? You've crunched the numbers with your best engineers and mathematicians. Do you know roughly the quantity of stone you're going to need to build such a monumental structure? By all calculations, you'll need over 2 million blocks of limestone retrieved from nearby quarries, hauled on wooden sleds up watered ramps to be finished and put into place. But as you look around in the twilight of that empty plateau, the magnitude of the job seems almost overwhelming. And yet glory awaits the completion of this unrivaled masterpiece.

You line up your thumb before your face with that North star, and before you leave, you offer a silent prayer to the gods for guidance, and protection, and safety–and to allow you to live to see the completion of this task. You have a little over 20 years.

Can you feel the weight of such an enormous task? It must have felt like being crushed under one of those limestone blocks. And yet...what if you *could* do it?

# How to Build a Pyramid

It's a truism that, to finish well, one must start well. With a project as ambitious as this, the earliest decisions and actions can make the difference between resounding success and crushing failure. We know that the building of Khufu's Great Pyramid was successful on a scale unmatched by any other edifice on earth for more than three millennia, and no other single structure has outlasted it, or likely ever will. The decisions made and the steps which Khufu took more than four millennia ago were the right ones. If Khufu wished to create a monument with an enduring sense of permanence, this would be it. So what were those decisions and those steps? We'll consider each of these in turn as we learn from the best how to build a pyramid.

## Choose the Right Man for the Job

In the brief imagination exercise above, I attempted to convey that choosing the right man is indispensable to success. Hindsight is always one hundred percent for us who look back from the vantage point of the future. We can easily say, *I knew all along that would work.* There were no such assurances before Khufu embarked on his ambitious plan, no matter how strong his belief in the soundness of it. All he had was the advice of his trusted officials and advisors–and, I believe, his capacity to be a good judge of character. There was no mistaking that good character was the primary requirement for this undertaking. There was no one whose resume included pyramid-building–nothing of this magnitude had ever been done before!

Khufu's choice of Hemiunu, thought to have been his nephew, to oversee the entire project from top to bottom proved to be the good first decision we discussed a moment ago. We don't know much about the man except that he was accomplished in several diverse administrative roles. He must have had the pharaoh's complete trust and confidence to be selected for a position of such consequence (Wilkinson, 2013). We must remember that the pyramid was not designed to serve as a giant memorial, like some elaborate, gargantuan tombstone. That sort of thought is merely the overlay of our 21st-century mindset upon a vastly different culture. Egyptian culture was obsessed with the Afterlife, and especially with the prospect of resurrection. No, the pyramids in general, and this Great Pyramid in particular, were not designed to be grave-markers—they were intended to be resurrection machines! Bob Brier emphasizes that "when the dead pharaoh was resurrected, as the religion of the ancient Egyptians foretold, his new self would travel to the Polar Star, situated directly north" (Brier & A Hoyt Hobbs, 2013, p. 218). Tom Wilkinson reminds us that "the efficiency of the pyramid as a means of resurrecting the king after his death depended on the accuracy of its orientation" (Wilkinson, 2013). The newly resurrected Khufu would, it seems, use the pyramid as an earthly guidepost, pointing his potentially disoriented new self to his new, eternal home.

There could be no mistakes and no margin of error when the pharaoh's eternal destiny hung in the balance. Khufu needed someone he could trust with his life—and so he chose Hemiunu. The result? We can say nothing about the pharaoh's potential, or actual spiritual resurrection, though we know that his physical remains have never been found. What is certain is that he could never have been misguided by an improperly oriented resurrection machine such as the Great Pyramid at Giza–Hemiunu accomplished its "alignment to true north with an error of only one-twentieth of a degree" (Wilkinson, Toby, 2015)!

## Pick the Site Carefully

Just as the wrong choice of overseer for such a grand project as Khufu's pyramid could spell disaster, so, too, could choosing the wrong site. After all, the platform for such a massive structure would need to be capable of supporting over 2 million stones, each weighing between one and two tons. That's more than 4,000,000 tons of limestone–a mind-boggling figure! But Khufu had chosen the best man for the job, and Hemiunu's choice of a platform for this monumental structure would be an excellent choice over the next 4,500 and more years. The Giza plateau contains a large vein of hard grey limestone, known by geologists as the Mokattam Formation.

It was upon this extremely stable bedrock that Hemiunu chose to erect the pyramid. The site had several other distinct advantages: it stood within a short distance of the step pyramids of Saqqara, visible to and from them as seemed appropriate for a royal monument; it was close to fast supplies of local building materials, notably softer limestone deposits which could be quarried and transported more quickly and easily to the plateau; there was room in the vicinity of the Giza plateau to erect what Bob Brier describes as a virtual Boomtown (2013) to house, feed, and care for the tens of thousands of workers who would spend the next 20 years building the pyramid. It was a relatively short four miles from the Giza plateau to the banks of the Nile. Though workers would have to excavate a canal to float supplies to the plateau from up the river, the location ensured that during the inundation every August and September, boats could reach the plateau's base easily, providing an uninterrupted supply chain for this massive undertaking. The digging of the canal necessitated the dredging of a harbor on the river and the building of docks to accommodate the increased number of boats and barges required.

**Find your Bearings**

As we noted earlier in this chapter, the orientation of the future pyramid needed to be exact. The resurrected life of the pharaoh himself depended on it! Suppose the engineers' calculations caused the pyramid to deviate by even a minuscule amount from true north. In that case, those deviations could be magnified in the finished structure to produce a pyramid that was unusable. According to the pharaoh's timeline, there would be no opportunity to build a second pyramid should the first fail to meet the exacting standards required by Egyptian religion. Unlike Zoser with his step pyramids at Saqqara, there would be no second chance.

There were several methods by which Egyptian engineers could determine precisely the orientation needed for the pyramid's foundation with fair precision. Each technique involved the position of the building relative to the north pole or star, which was always visible to the Egyptians. This was the same polar star to which if the building program was more successful, Koufos resurrected spirit would fly. And the first method of determining orientation two true north involves the use of a plumbline. Two stars rotate in a regular pattern around the celestial polar star. It was discovered that when those two stars are perfectly vertically aligned with the polar star and a plumbline suspended in the plane of their orientation, true north could be established as the basis to orient the building. Another method involved the planting of a stick so that it would cast no shadow at noon. If engineers marked the stick's shadow at a specific interval before and after noon, the point halfway between those marks indicated true north. A third method involved building a temporary wall with its top edge as level as possible and facing as closest possible to the north. The builder would observe the rising of a particular star, mark its position on the top of the wall, and later make a similar mark at the place where that same star set, the point halfway between was sure to be as close as possible to true north.

What is remarkable is that the orientation of a massive structure like the Great Pyramid, which is so critical, in the Egyptian worldview, to the king's future, could be made using rudimentary tools and methods. The Egyptians did not need advanced mathematical principles or the assistance (as some have claimed) of aliens! Everything they needed was within their grasp.

## Make it Level, Larry!

To be fair, there was no manual written in Egyptian or any other language to instruct architects, engineers, and builders in the knottier points of pyramid construction, such as guaranteeing a level foundation that would measure 756 feet square at its base. Nor, I suspect, would such an instruction manual be appreciated or even needed. Nevertheless, through a process of trial and error, Zoser managed, within his lifetime, to build a step pyramid that has stood the test of time and still stands today. And while, for at least the first three dynasties of the Early Kingdom, Egyptian civilization still had one foot firmly planted in the lower Neolithic age, it is beyond dispute that they were fundamentally masters of stone. Thus, it is not surprising that their most iconic structures were raised during this period. Moreover, the sheer number of Egyptian tombs, temples, and even the pyramids scattered throughout the land is a testament to their deep knowledge of and facility with stoneworking.

It should come as no surprise, then, that the elevation of the Great Pyramid from corner to corner, over a length of 756 feet, deviates by less than one inch (Brier & A Hoyt Hobbs, 2013, p. 219). The question remains: How did they accomplish such a feat? The answer may be more simple than you think. Brier and Hobbs (2013) have suggested that the engineers may have cut a shallow trough around the pyramid's perimeter and filled it with water to function as a giant level. Workers would excavate any spot where the ground was unlevel until the level was achieved.

## Get the Teams Together

By now, you may be wondering what sort of workforce was needed to build the great pyramid of Giza? First, we've considered the raw numbers of material and the pace at which the pyramid would need to be created: over two million stones, weighing anywhere from one to two tons each on average, to be placed at an average rate of 30 blocks per hour, seven days a week, 350 days a year, for 20 years. Many of the workers employed in this venture were farmers who couldn't work their fields for weeks or months after the inundation. They constituted a transient workforce since they must have returned home to plant their fields once the waters had receded. Pharaoh's recruitment officers roamed the land enlisting those strong and able-bodied enough to endure the backbreaking work of pyramid construction. Egyptologists are of two minds regarding the nature and outcome of this recruitment process. Bob Brier (Brier & Λ Hoyt Hobbs, 2013) believes that the workforce pressed into service for Pharaoh was composed primarily of freemen and patriots willing to serve their king and their country—more like a partnership than a proscription. However, Toby Wilkinson sees a darker side to the workforce management of ancient Egypt. Imagined living conditions in the pyramid town adjacent to the Giza plateau, and similar pyramid towns built during later dynasties, suggest that far from being willing participants, the workers who worked 10 hours a day seven days a week to make the pyramids did not enlist but were instead drafted into a rigorous and disciplined working structure. They were provided with crude dormitory accommodation and seem to have eaten communally. The evidence of refuse dumps from these pyramid towns indicates that food was a significant preoccupation for these workers, understandable because of the nature of the work they performed. Perhaps the men were not slaves as portrayed in classic movies, but again, there was likely not a volunteer arrangement sealed with a handshake.

I refer again to Toby Wilkinson, who has done the math of which I speak. I suspect that his calculations for the size of the workforce and organizational structure are based upon the sleeping capacity of dormitories in the pyramid town. A bunkhouse or dormitory can sleep up to 40 men (20 on each side of the long building). So then, it is likely that the basic workforce unit consists of a team of 20 men with one team leader. Teams will compete against one another and pace one another, enabling greater productivity. Ten teams comprise a division or, in Greek, a phyle. Five phyles would make up a gang of 1000 workers, and two gangs with unique identities and comraderies made a crew—the largest unit. The larger units of such a workforce are allegedly attested in surviving inscriptions, but Wilkinson does not identify the source of these.

He goes on to say, "calculations and practical experiments have shown that just two crews, or

4000 men, would have been sufficient to quarry, haul, and set in place more than 2 million stone blocks used to build the pyramid" (Wilkinson, 2013).

Wilkinson suggests that perhaps the same size of the workforce would have been needed to construct and maintain the vast ramps, leading from the main quarry to the pyramid and then up the sides of the monument as it grew in height; however, Brier and Hobbs dismiss the outside pyramid ramp idea as being impractical and costly both in time and resources. Briar and Hobbs' suggestion is that workers may have built a shorter, more shallow ramp to reach the first few courses as the pyramid grew but that afterward, the stones would have been moved up ramps on the inside of the pyramid structure, expanding the hallways as they move forward to each successive course. Indeed, this idea is intriguing. Wilkinson discusses the "army of workers" working behind the scenes to keep the machine running, as it were. He concludes with this statement, that "the number of people employed at any one time on the pyramid project may not have risen much beyond 10,000 at any one time" (Wilkinson, 2013). If pyramid construction took place 350 days out of a year and if sickness, injury, and death were as significant as they may appear, Wilkinson's numbers may be conservative. A workforce of free men and patriots? Given the nature of the work, I am not sure, but that may be a rosier picture than the reality, driven by a divine imperative of absolute and unquestioned obedience to a god-king.

# Chapter 7: I'm Not Your Mummy!

As we have seen in previous chapters, the history of ritual care for the bodies of the deceased has a long history, stretching back into neolithic and even Palaeolithic times. You may remember that I raised the intriguing question: Why is it that many human remains were uncovered in the Nile Valley in shallow burial pits in the sand, curled into a contracted or fetal position, laying on their left sides, with their heads pointing south and their faces pointing to the west? I mentioned then that we might never know the answer to the why of that seemingly ritual behavior. But there can be no coincidence in the repeated performance of that minor ritual. Perhaps it is part of the human psyche to treat the dead with a measure of reverence and respect. But, of course, that is not necessarily true when the deceased was one's enemy. There is evidence, relatively recent in the archeological record, of bodies having been thrown into a mass pit or grave together, having had their throats slit most unceremoniously. Such instances might represent rudimentary human sacrifice, but the motivations will remain forever hidden since neither the dead in those pits nor their killers can reach out from their graves to enlighten us.

Nonetheless, in classic post-unification Egypt, there is a progression in burial rights until, as Bob Brier has said, "preserving the physical body after death became, over the centuries, a kind of Egyptian industry" (Brier & Hoyt Hobbs, 2013). All the instances, in Paleolithic and Neolithic times, of sandpit burial failed to preserve the body as well as its attendants may have desired. Of course, the dry sand would serve as a desiccant to dehydrate the body and create what we think of as "natural" mummies. By 3500 BC, however, as we saw in a previous chapter, thought had been given to treatments to preserve the body, such as wrapping in strips of linen cloth and covering with fur, the first instance in the archeological record of intentional mummification. Now, this was nothing like the detailed and meticulous procedures which developed in civilized Egypt. But it does point tantalizingly forward to the early days of united Egypt when burials became more elaborate. As with other cultures to come, bodies were placed in rock-cut tombs much like the mausoleums of today. Still, these bodies would soon decompose without the benefit of sand's dehydrating properties, especially in a hot climate. It became clear to the Egyptians that some artificial means were necessary to preserve the deceased's body before burial. They believed that the spirit of the deceased would require that body to carry them on their journey through the Underworld, hopefully–though by no means certainly–to eternity in paradise, called the Field of Reeds.

In ancient Egypt, embalming shops were situated on the east side of the Nile river and burial sites on the west. This practice was a deliberate and strategic choice, necessitating a ritual boat ride first toward the east and then back across the river to the burial site on the west bank. The intent of this was to symbolize the deceased individual's journey through the Underworld toward resurrection in the west. Thus, a family who had no means to provide their own boat would need to rent a special funerary boat to transport their loved one's remains to the embalming shop. Then, in a scene reminiscent of the cultures of the Middle East in our day, female mourners would be commissioned to lament the passing of the soul into the far world. They would weep and wail, and in an eastern Mediterranean style, pour sand on their heads in mock remorse.

The mummification process involved several well-orchestrated steps:

removal of the moist organs, those most likely to cause decomposition

removal of the organs from the torso to be stored in special containers

preparing the body with a mixture of various salts to dry the body completely

washing and packing of the body cavities, specifically the abdomen and the chest

padding of the face with linen in the cheeks and under the eyelids

anointing the body with precious oils and lotions while a priest recited prayers the extraordinarily meticulous and painstaking bandaging of the body to prepare for the journey to the underworld.

Let's look at each of these steps in a little more detail to appreciate the process.

The first step of the mummification process removed the soft tissues, which would cause the body to decompose quickly. And as is true of each step in the process, the techniques used and the extent to which they were employed were tailored to suit the budget of the surviving family members. The most costly method to accomplish this first step involved inserting a long, needle-like instrument through the nostril to pierce the brain cavity, followed by a thin tool resembling a coat hanger or perhaps a crochet hook, when rotated, would break the brain into pieces. Next, the corpse was placed in a prone position so that the brain matter would drain through the nostrils. Egyptians gave no thought to preserving the brain because the seat of the soul, in their belief, was not the brain but the heart.

The next organs to be removed were the stomach, liver, spleen, and intestines, all removed through a tiny incision in the abdomen on the left side. The heart was left untouched and in place. It was believed in the Egyptian worldview to be the center and seat of human thought. Since the deceased would have to remember and recite specific magic spells on the other side to be reanimated, the heart must stay where it was. The other organs, once removed, were placed into particular jars, each of whose lids were carved in the shape of one of the four sons of Horus: Mesti, with a human head; Duamutef, who resembled a jackal; Hapy, represented by a baboon; and Qebesenef, a hawk.

Before the embalmers sealed the jars, they poured a preservative liquid over the organs inside. They sealed the jars while priests recited prayers.

The next step in the process was the preparation of the body for drying. And this involved covering the body with a naturally occurring alkaline mixture called natron. The salt mixture consisted of sodium bicarbonate, sodium chloride, and sodium carbonate. Depending upon the size of the body, after the embalmers shoveled 600 pounds and possibly more of natron over the body to cover it entirely, the body was left to desiccate for 40 days.

At the end of that time, the body was removed from the natron. Its cavities were cleansed with wine and aromatic spices and packed with linen soaked in resin to preserve the body's natural contours. Of course, cheaper burials involved cheaper stuffing, typically sawdust and bags of onions. The cheeks and nose sockets are padded with linen as well so that the face maintained a lifelike appearance. Finally, the body was anointed twice with oils containing a mixture of frankincense, cedar oil, Syrian balsam, and oil of Libya. As the oils were being administered, a priest would recite specific prayers. The wrapping of the deceased body was intricate and purposeful. Bandages could be provided by the family and were usually scraps of linen or the bedding of the deceased. These were torn into strips 4 inches wide, and as much as 15 feet long, and rolled to be applied according to a fixed ceremony and ritual. Each finger and toe was wrapped separately, then the head bound tightly so that one could recognize the contours of the face. This was governed by strict and unwavering rituals and presided over by priests to ensure that the individual could see and breathe in the afterlife. The extremities were last to be bandaged. Usually, magic amulets were woven into the wrappings for protection until the body's resurrection.

The most crucial resurrection ritual awaited the deceased's return with their family and friends to the tomb on the west bank of the Nile. Once servants had stocked the tomb with furniture, food, and other necessities for their family member's journey through the Afterlife, a highly ritualized drama was enacted before the grave, officiated by a priest who dictated the order of service. This was the opening of the mouth ceremony as summarized by Bob Brier, an expert in the lost art of mummification:

The ground on which the play was to be performed was purified with water from four vases representing the four corners of the earth. Actresses, often members of the family, portrayed Isis and her sister Nephthys; males acted as the guardians of Horus and a central character called "The-son-who-loved-him." After incense was lit and various gods invoked, a calf was slaughtered to commemorate the battle in which Horus avenged the murder of his father,

Osiris. (In the continuation of the Isis and Osiris myth, Seth's conspirators, attempting to escape the avenging Horus by changing into various animals, were caught by Horus and decapitated.) Special animals were ritually killed, including two bulls (one for the north and one for the south), gazelles, and ducks. One leg from the bull of the south was cut off and, along with its heart, offered to the mummy (Brier & Hoyt Hobbs, 2013, p. 65).

The final step in this ceremony involved a priest touching the deceased on the mouth with a special implement while reciting the following prayer, after which the tomb was sealed, and the funeral party shared a meal:

Thy mouth was closed, but I have set in order for thee thy mouth and thy teeth.
I open for thee thy mouth, I open for thee thy two eyes. I have opened thy mouth
with the instrument of Anubis, with the iron implement with which the mouths
of the gods were opened....
You shall walk and speak, your body shall be with the great company of the gods....
You are young again, you live again.

You are young again, you live again. (Brier &
Hoyt Hobbs, 2013)

# Conclusion

The history of ancient Egypt began with conflict, and with a king who unified the Two Lands, creating a civilization that would endure for 3,000 years. It ended with war, and with a queen whose death was the dissolution of that 3,000-year-old civilization. Between these two markers, we've witnessed the birth, maturing, and decline of earth's second-oldest civilization. We have seen Neolithic hunter-gatherers gradually exchange their nomadic ways for a sedentary, agrarian social structure. Tribes have become villages; villages, cities; and cities, a nation. A tribal chieftain has become the ruler of the Two Lands of Upper and Lower Egypt. His successors would build tombs–called pyramids– on a scale unrivaled in history until the 14th century BCE. Stories shared around the flickering hearth of a tiny wattle and daub hut became a religion that defines a civilization. That civilization's rulers aspired to divinity, calling themselves sons or daughters of a deity. The gods themselves dominated every aspect of ancient Egyptian society, presiding over life and especially over the death of its people. And isolated, insulated Egypt grew in military might and by territorial expansion until it became the Egyptian Empire, rivaling Babylonia and Assyria for world power and domination. Eventually, that empire faded and ultimately disappeared.

Yet the river, *iteru*, the Nile, lives on. Egypt is no longer Kemet, the Black Land. The inundation of Hapy no longer reaches the Nile Valley, its way barred by the Aswan High Dam. But late every summer, as has happened for thousands of years before, towering storm clouds rush in from the Atlantic Ocean and disgorge their contents in a deluge of water over the Ethiopian highlands, filling the Blue Nile to overflowing in a roaring torrent that rushes on as if unaware that ancient Egypt, who's lifeblood it ever was, is no more. The one who has ears to hear, let him hear–hear, and remember.

# About the Author

At History Brought Alive, we share one passion: ancient history and mythology. And we have one mission: to present you, the reader, with meticulously researched, expertly crafted, and thoroughly enjoyable works that will ignite that same passion in you! We curate the information in our books not only to provide you with the essential facts but to create an *experience*. We want you to see, feel, and hear as the history and mythology of ancient civilizations are "brought alive" in your mind's eye. Our books will become welcome additions to your library collection, trusted works to which you will return time after time. And future generations will be informed and entertained by these timeless histories and mythologies of long ago.

# Free Bonus from HBA: Ebook Bundle

Greetings!

First of all, thank you for reading our books. As fellow passionate readers of history and mythology we aim to create the very best books for our readers.

Now, we invite you to join our VIP list. As a welcome gift we offer the History & Mythology Ebook Bundle below for free. Plus you can be the first to receive new books and exclusives! Remember it's 100% free to join.

Simply follow the link below to join.

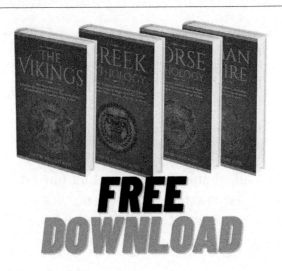

# References

Adams, J. (2021). *Africa during the last 150,000 years.* Ornl.gov. https://www.esd.ornl.gov/projects/qen/nercAF RICA.html

Bell, B. (1970). The Oldest Records of the Nile Floods. *The Geographical Journal, 136*(4), 569. https://doi.org/10.2307/1796184

Brier, B. (1999). *The history of ancient Egypt: Course guide.* The Great Courses. http://www.thegreatcourses.com

Brier, B., & A Hoyt Hobbs. (2013). Ancient Egypt: Everyday life in the land of the Nile. Sterling.

deMenocal, P. B., & Tierney, J. E. (2012). Green Sahara: African humid periods paced by earth's orbital changes. *Nature Education Knowledge, 3*(10), 12.

Edwards, A. B. (2014). *A thousand miles up the Nile* (2nd ed.). Big Byte Books.

Eltahir, N. (2021, January 4). Egypt eyes slow return for tourism after revenues dive in 2020. *Reuters*. www.reuters.com

Feeney, J. (2006). The last Nile flood. *Saudi Aramco World*, *57*(3), 24–33. archive.aramcoworld.com.

Geggel, L. (2017, March 17). *"Gilded Lady" and other exquisite mummies on display in NYC*. Live Science; Future Plc. http://livescience.com

Gemmill, P. F. (1928). Egypt Is the Nile. *Economic Geography*, *4*(3), 295. https://doi.org/10.2307/140298

Godfrey Mugoti. (2009). *Africa (a-z)*. Lulu Com.

Haney, L. S. (n.d.). Egypt and the Nile. *Carnegie Museum of Natural History*. Retrieved September 18, 2021, from http://www.carnegiemnh.org

Harari, Y. N. (2014). *Sapiens: A brief history of humankind*. http://www.amazon.ca

Harvey Gallagher Cox. (2013). The secular city: Secularization and urbanization in theological perspective. Princeton Univ. Press.

Heath, J. M. (2021). Before the pharaohs: Exploring the archaeology of stone age Egypt. Pen and Sword Books. http://www.amazon.ca

*Herodotus: II 19-31.* (2020). Uoregon.edu. https://darkwing.uoregon.edu/~klio/tx/gr/H-NILE.HTM

*Hymn to the Nile flood.* (2002). Www.ucl.ac.uk; University College London. https://www.ucl.ac.uk/museums-static/digitalegypt/literature/floodtransl.html

Keding, B. (2000). New data on the Holocene occupation of the Wadi Howar region (Eastern Sahara/Sudan). *Studies in African Archaeology*, 7, 89–104.

Liu, S., Lu, P., Liu, D., Jin, P., & Wang, W. (2009). Pinpointing the sources and measuring the lengths of the principal rivers of the world. *International Journal of Digital Earth*, 2(1), 80–87. https://doi.org/10.1080/17538940902746082

Mark, J. J. (2016a, April 14). *Egyptian Gods - The Complete List*. World History Encyclopedia. https://worldhistory.org/article/885/egyptian-gods----the-complete-list/

Mark, J. J. (2016b, October 13). *Ancient Egyptian Government*. World History Encyclopedia. https://www.worldhistory.org/Egyptian_Govern ment

Marlow, H. (2007). The Lament over the River Nile—Isaiah xix 5-10 in Its Wider Context. *Vetus Testamentum*, *57*(2), 229–242. https://doi.org/10.1163/156853307x183721

Maslin, M., & Leakey, R. E. (2019). The cradle of humanity: How the changing landscape of Africa made us so smart. Oxford University Press.

Mertz, B. (2009a). Red land, black land : Daily life in ancient Egypt. HarperCollins e-books.

Mertz, B. (2009b). *Temples, tombs, and hieroglyphs: A popular history of ancient Egypt* (2nd Revised, Updated Ed.). HarperCollins e-books.

*Mousterian Pluvial*. (2021, February 17). Wikipedia. https://en.wikipedia.org/w/index.php?title=Mo usterian_Pluvial&oldid=1007401031

Pinch, G. (2004). Egyptian mythology: A guide to the gods, goddesses, and traditions of ancient Egypt. Oxford University Press.

Sandford, K. S., & Arkell, W. J. (n.d.). *Prehistoric survey of Egypt and western Asia: Paleolithic man and the Nile-Faiyum Divide* (J. H. Breasted, Ed.; Vol. 1). The University of Chicago Oriental Institute Publications. http://www.oi.uchicago.edu (Original work published 1929)

Shaw, G. J. (2014). The Egyptian myths: A guide to the ancient gods and legends. Thames & Hudson.

Shaw, I. (Ed.). (2000). *The Oxford history of ancient Egypt.* Oxford University Press.

Smithsonian's National Museum of Natural History. (2010, March). *The Smithsonian Institution's Human Origins Program.* The Smithsonian Institution's Human Origins Program. http://humanorigins.si.edu

Stanley, J.-D., & Wedl, S. E. (2021). Significant depositional changes offshore the Nile Delta in late third millennium BCE: relevance for Egyptology. *E&G Quaternary Science Journal,*

*70*(1), 83–92. https://doi.org/10.5194/egqsj-70-83-2021

Taylor, J. H. (2001). *Death and the afterlife in ancient Egypt*. University Of Chicago Press.

*Terra Amata (archaeological site)*. (2021, June 5). Wikipedia. https://en.wikipedia.org/w/index.php?title=Terra_Amata_(archaeological_site)&oldid=1027028445

University of Cologne. (2021, June 14). *Climate conditions during the migration of Homo sapiens out of Africa reconstructed*. Sciencedaily.com; ScienceDaily. http://www.sciencedaily.com/releases/2021/06/210614153909.htm

Vermeersch, P. M., & Van Neer, W. (2015). Nile behaviour and Late Palaeolithic humans in Upper Egypt during the Late Pleistocene. *Quaternary Science Reviews, 130*, 155–167. https://doi.org/10.1016/j.quascirev.2015.03.025

Wilkinson, Toby. (2015). The Nile: Travelling downriver through Egypt's past and present. New York Vintage Departures.

Wilkinson, R. H. (2003). The complete gods and goddesses of ancient Egypt. Thames & Hudson Inc.

Wilkinson, T. H. (2013). *The rise and fall of ancient Egypt*. Random House Trade Paperbacks.

Printed in Great Britain
by Amazon

33275621R00119

GRIN - Verlag für akademische Texte

Der GRIN Verlag mit Sitz in München hat sich seit der Gründung im Jahr 1998 auf die Veröffentlichung akademischer Texte spezialisiert. Die Verlagswebseite www.grin.com ist für Studenten, Hochschullehrer und andere Akademiker die ideale Plattform, ihre Fachtexte, Studienarbeiten, Abschlussarbeiten oder Dissertationen einem breiten Publikum zu präsentieren.

**Dokument Nr. V170410 aus dem GRIN Verlagsprogramm**

Christian Röse

# Inequalities in Health

**What inequalities exist and why this is seen as a social problem**

GRIN Verlag

Bibliografische Information der Deutschen Nationalbibliothek: Die Deutsche Bibliothek
verzeichnet diese Publikation in der Deutschen Nationalbibliografie; detaillierte bibliografische Daten sind im Internet über http://dnb.d-nb.de/ abrufbar.


1. Auflage 2010
Copyright © 2010 GRIN Verlag
http://www.grin.com/
Druck und Bindung: Books on Demand GmbH, Norderstedt Germany
ISBN 978-3-640-89248-8

School of Sociology & Social Policy

# Inequalities in Health

*What inequalities exist and why this is seen as a social problem*

Module Title: Health: Theory, Policy and Practice

Student: Christian Röse

*January 13th, 2011*

## Table of Contents

## Abstract

This essay is about inequities in health and to what extent they are seen as a social problem. In the first part the measurements for "inequalities" and "health" are clarified. Applying these measurements, the second part highlights currently existing inequalities in health in the UK today. The last part of the essay assesses the question why inequalitiesstem from social differences and what makes them problematic.

## How to assess Inequalities in Health

In 1977, the working group of inequalities in health, known as the "Black Group", was given the tas k to review inf ormation a bout differences in h ealth status betw een t he socia l classes;...,' (Black, 198 0). M ore t han t hirty years have passed since that first official assessment of the impact of soci al differences on the status of health. But still the question to reveal inequalities in health (the first part of the essay) is the same.

### Concept of Measuring Health

Our understanding of what we perceive as health and ill-health is not a stable construct. It rather has v aried t hroughout the past and a ccording t o exp erience, so ciety a nd sit uational factors and each subgroups of the s ociety will have a slightl y different focus about how to understand health (Bl ack, 1980). In order to a ssess health and differences in heal th, our subjective const ructs and understandings of health firs t need to be t ransferred in to measurable, operational terms.

According to the Black report, the most common measurements of health are 'mortality rate, prevalence or incid ence morbidi ty rates, si ckness-absence rates an d restri cted-activity rates'(Black, 1980). This essay will mainly focus on mortality rates which are in line with th e Black report and a very familiar form of m easurement (Black, 1980). How ever each measurement has its own limitation and it should be mentioned that the major drawbacks of mortality rate is that it tends to underes timate the prevalence of chronic illness and other disease w hich in fluence human "well-being". T herefore it is critical to keep in mind other forms of as sessment and combine th ose, f or example a r eflection of social, em otional a nd physical functions (Black, 1980) such as the m easurement of life satis faction included into this analysis.

### Concept of Inequalities

The term *inequality in health is* not simply a question of assessment as clarified above. Once we have identifi ed how to m easure health, we need to clarify w hat is understood by *inequalities*.

The Black r eport dif ferentiates b etween *inequalities* and *differences*. Differences such as in race, sex or age are na turally occurring and th erefore not seen as pr oblematic. In equalities however ar e 'br ought about b y s ocial ... or ganizations a nd ... tend to b e r egarded as

undesirable or of doubtful validity by gr oups of soci ety` (Black, 1980). Consequently it can be said t hat th e Black repor t shapes t he term both as r esulting fr om *socio-economic*differences and as *morally not neutral*. This specifi c meaning s hould be carried in mind throughout the text. However not everybody appreciates the rather loaded and slightly ambiguous meaning of the term. Therefore the World Heal th Org anization rath er proposed the term `i nequities` for in equalities whi ch ar e unjusti fiable a nd undesirable ( Macintyre, 2002).

## Concept of Social Class

*Why is social class used as a measure and how is it constructed?*

After assess ing how to measur e he alth we no w ne ed to d efine t he se cond v ariable, a measure of inequalities. As the discussion on inequalities above suggests, it ought to b e some kind of social-economic construct. In B ritain, there has been a long tradition of measuring inequalities in health in terms of *occupational class* or status. This is dating back as long as the seventeenth centur y and wa s rather adopted by Black in 1980 then newly constructed (Macintyre, 2002).The widespread use of occupation can be accounted for by its comparable easy usage. As Black explains it,

> `inequalities are diffi cult to measur e and tren ds in inequalities in the di stribution of income an d wealth , for example, cannot be related to i ndicators of health, except indirectly. Partly f or re asons of convenience, therefore, occupational st atus or class (which is correlated closely with various other measures of inequality), is used as the principal indicator of social inequalities ....' (Black, 1980).

Occupational status is theref ore strongly related to a wide r ange of other factors a ssociated with inequal ities such as housing, education, i ncome-level and life-style. It will hence be used in th e analysis. The Regis trar Ge neral's Social Class (RGSC) of socio-economic classification is applied, althoug h since 2001 t he new N ational Statis tics Soci o-Economic Classification (NS-SEC) , with up to eight occupational categ ories, h as been int roduced. (Office of National Statistics, 2010)

However in order to ensure that pas t statistics are correctly incorporate into the analysis of long-term trends, the following "old" classification system is used:

I.  Professional (e.g. accountant, doctor, lawyer) (5%)

II.  Intermediate (e.g. manager, schoolteacher, nurse) (18%)

III. i) Skilled non-manual (e.g. clerical worker, secretary, shop assistant) (12%)

      ii) Skilled manual (e.g. bus driver, butcher, coal face worker, carpenter) (38%)

IV.  Partly skilled (e.g. agricultural worker, bus conductor, postman) (18%)

V.  Unskilled (e.g. labourer, cleaner, dock worker) (9%)

(Source: Black, 1980 p.15)

## Existing Inequalities

As we have defined the operational terms, we will now cont inue to reveal existing inequalities.

> "There is so much evidence demonstrating d ifferences i n mort ality and morbidi ty between th e social cla sses ... tha t it is difficult to sele ct from evid ence. Th ese differences are well known." (Brotherston, 1975 quoted in Macintyre, 2002)

This quote was used as the opening sentence of a lecture on inequalities of health in 1975. Although th e phras e seems out dated t oday, i t clearl y an d sadly is not! Ther e is a hug e amount of r esearch about social class differen ces in r elation to h ealth. However th is article puts a lot of emphasis on using *recent* da ta and up -to-date in formation. On important construct needs to be introduced for a better understanding of th e a nalysis: In Nov ember 2004 the Department of Health in troduced the *Spearhead Group* which consists of the Local Authority areas that have the worst health and deprivation indicators compared to the rest of England. It contains 70 Local Authorities and the 62 Primary Care Trust areas they belong to. In total, the Spearhead group contains 28% of the population of England, more than a quarter (Health Inequality Unit, 2007, Department of Health, 2006).

### Life Expectancy

The first in dicator f or i nequalities i s the ag e p eople are expected to reach.Nationwide lif e expectancy has increas ed in the la st 20 year s for both men and wom en and in cluding th e Spearhead areas. Th ere has bee n an incre ase of 3,1 year s for males and of 2 ,1 years for females in the population between 1995-'97 and 2005-'07. However the improvement in life expectancy is unequally distributed . For S pearhead ar eas there is less increas e in lif e expectancy. Especially women in the Sp earhead group h ave a l ower level of im provement with only 1.9 years extra and with 2.9 years fo r males in the Spe arhead areas ( Department

of Health, 2 009). Although the di fference of 0 ,2 years is only a sligh t devia tion from th e national trend, the gap in life expectancy between disadvantages areas and the rest remains wide with 2 % for mal es and by 11 % for females in 2004-'06 (Department of Health, 2009 ). This trend under pins the existing variation between socia l grou ps, displayed in the gr aph below, with peopl e fr om the pr ofessional occupational class having the hig hest life expectancy with a descending tr end according to th e occupational classes (D epartment of Health, 200 9, Heal th Inequality Unit, 2007 ). However t here a re s ome ex ceptions to this trend. Between 1997-2001 life expectancy for man increased especially for group I.,"manual worker", which closed the difference to the non-manual group (Department of Health, 2009). For woman, occupational group seems to be less influential as ʽestimates of life expectancy increased by a similar amoun t for those classified to non-manual an d manual occupati onsʽ

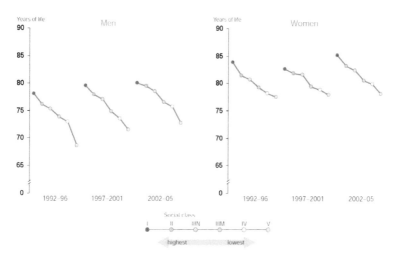

(Department of Health, 2009).

Figure1: Life expectancyatbirthbysocialclass (England and Wales, 1992-2005)

(Source: Department of Health, 2009 p. 117)

## Infant Mortality

Infant m ortality ra te is seen as a ʽgood in dicator of th e health of a societyʽ; the hig hly emotional componen t of infant dea th makes them especi ally critical and ʽeach avoidable death is one too manyʽ. Infant mortality also heavily triggers the low life expectancy rates in the Spearhead group (Health Inequality Unit, 2007).Overall the Department of Health

suggests in various publications that there has been a significant improvement in infant mortality over the past 10 years and that all social groups have been affected by the improving trend (Department of Health, 2009). Please note, that unlike life expectancy rates, infant mortality is displayed in NS-SEC with three groups of the infants' parents. Those are I. "Managerial and professionals occupations", II. "Intermediate occupations" and III. "Routine and manual occupations". Further the groups "Other" (student, unemployed or people who never worked) and "Sole registrations" (children registered by the mother only) are added to the analysis (Office of National Statistics, 2010, Department of Health, 2009).

As the Department of Health relieved in 2008 (in the Status Report on the Program for Action) infant mortality was at an historic low level. Between 2005-'07, 4.7 infants per 1,000 live births died for all those in England with a valid socio-economic group compared to 5.6 per 1,000 in 1995-'97. (Department of Health, 2008). However, as can be drawn from the table below (Department of Health, 2009), there are still large differences between the occupational groups. For the routine and manual group there seems to be a recent narrowing in the gap between the rest of the population. In the last two years of assessment, 2004 to 2006, infant mortality rate was 17% higher in the routine and manual group than for the rest of the population, compared to of 18% in 2003-'05 and 19% in 2002-'04. However if evaluated against a difference of only 13% in 1997-'99 (Department of Health, 2009), it is questionable if there is much of an improvement. Further the disadvantage of the Routine and Manual group can be expressed in total numbers. In 2004 to 2006 there were 8,674 infant deaths in total. The Routine and Manual group accounted for 43% of them, creating a rate of 5.6 deaths per 1,000 live births. This is higher than the rate of 4.8 deaths per 1,000 for the other occupational groups combined (Health Inequality Unit, 2007). In the diagram below the group "Other "displays the highest mortality rate. However in total this group accounted for only 9.4 per cent of the deaths in 2004-'06 (Department of Health, 2009).

Figure 2: Infant mortality rate by socio-economic group (England and Wales, 1996-2006)

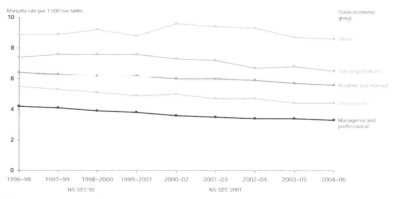

(Source: Department of Health, 2009 p.119)

## Life Satisfaction

As mentioned in the introduction a measure of other factors besides mortality rates is critical in order to achieve an overview on existing inequalities. Therefore a measure of self-reported life satisfaction is included which was carried out by the Department of Environment, Food and Rural Affairs in 2007. Participants rated their life satisfaction on a scale from 1, least satisfied, to 10, most satisfied. They found that `approximately three-quarter (73per cent) of the people in England rated their satisfaction with life as 7 or more out of 10`as depict in the graph below. In general there were high differences between both occupational group and age.

People in unskilled jobs, on state pension or unemployed were less satisfied with all aspects of their life compared to the other groups. On the other hand those people were more likely than average to have experienced negative feelings as depression, unsafe and lonely in the two weeks prior to the survey. On the othe    r hand people in skilled jobs were had experienced feelings of happiness, energy and engagement with their activities in the same time period.When looking at the satisfaction rating, differences between occupational classes can be seen. There is a "social grading" applied in the given graph, which is determined by occupation. For that, Group AB with jobs like doctors, accountants, nurses or police officers, have an average satisfaction rating of 7.6. If compared to group E, which are unemployed,

state pensioners or casual labours (rating 6.7) there is a decreasing trend. Ratings of a scale of 7 or 8, which are seen as having a satisfied life, were significantly less in this gr oup, but ratings of 5, bei ng n either sati sfied nor unsatis fied, were more common than in group AB (Department of Health, 2009). It remains difficu lt to analys e the numbers in the s ame way as with e.g. infant mortality. Still a trend in differences in life satisfaction is seen. Besides the life satisf action, so cial differences can also be seen in how pe ople e xperience t heir own health. People in higher social clas ses generally consider their current health to be better. Further 76 % of those in a higher social class also expected to be in good health over a period as long as 10 years, compared to only 53% in the lowest social class (National Health Service, 2 004). This a nd th e satis faction ra tings clarify that inequaliti es do not only have impact on physical health but, maybe to a similar degree, al so on psy chological health. The reverse relationship holds true as well. There is a causal relationship betw een psychological life stress factors and poor health, as specifically chronic stress lowers the body's ability of regeneration and defence (Wilkinson,1996).

Figure3: Self-reportedlifesatisfactionbysocial grade (England, 2007)

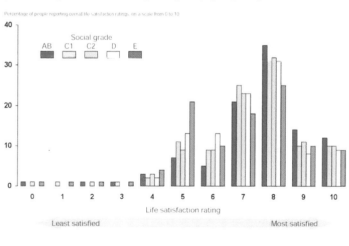

(Source: Department of Health, 2009 p.111)

## Conclusion

The heal th of th e popu lation has s ignificantly i mproved ov er the last  10 years, a nd this applies mu ch the same for th  e disadvant aged grou ps and areas , a s measured  by life expectancy and infant mortality (Department of Health, 2009). Although the infant mortality rates have declined, there is still n eed for improvem ent. On the  one hand ` each avoidable death is one too many and the number of pre- term babies is still too high`. And on the other hand, beside infant mortality, there are still a hig h number of children  with long-term health  conditions which em  bodies hug e emotional and finan cial burd ens for the families as  well as for  the govern ment and  society (Health Inequ ality Unit, 2007). A n important part of social inequalit y is the psyc hological impact of it, which has a life-long effect. This impact should not be underestimated.

## Inequalities as a Social Problem

Having assessed examples of t he  existing inequalities in the UK today,  we now turn to the question wh y these dif ferences are  seen as a  social probl em. At first  it is explained why inequalities are seen as a*social* issue, rather than an individual.

Much information can be found by looking at the results of the different reports on inequality in health. All docum entation show similar caus es. Starting with the Black Report (1 980), ɑ causal link  was seen between soci al and ec onomic factors and ill  health. Namel y, those factors were income, un employment, poor envi ronment, poor housing and educa tion (Black, 1980).  The same results were    confirmed by  the Health  Divide (198 7) an d t he Ach eson Report (1998). Out o f those f actors, the m ain causes of inequalities in  health were poverty and ed ucation. Th e dif ference be tween t he r ich and th  e po or in a coun  try and th e differences  between hi gher  or lo wer e ducation ar e so cially influ enced,  constructed an d maintained. This is why also their impact on health is regarded as a  *social* problem.A further influence stems from the role of the NHS. It has  been shown that the impact of the NHS t o health differences is relatively  l ow, leaving  the reasons for in equalities to  other, so cial, problems (Department of Health, 2008).

In general, nowadays a g rater de al of at tention is dev oted to  the social an d psy chological consequences of low incom e. As the living stan dards have improved throughout the society, the effects of material privation are drastically reduced. Poverty is no longer seen as absolute (material privation) but as relative, compared to the rest of the society. Further the impact of poverty is redefined as ´social  exclusion´ (Wil kinson, 200 5). This clearly shows  the s ocial

implication of low occupational groups.As a conc   lusion, it can be said that inequalities i    n health are seen as being social in their origin.

What still needs to be    assessed is the questi on why thos e differences are (automatically) regarded as *problematic*.For most of us, inequalities are intuitively seen as unfair, wrong and problematic. This is especially true  when they are itemized by social class as in the  previous analysis. But why exactly are differences in health seen as a problem, while other differences in society such as income level or education level are more readily accepted and less viewed as problematic?

Obviously, a major reas on is the o utcome ( or the cons equences) of in equalities in health . Differences in the life expectancy means ´loosing loved ones earlier´ for a lower social group (Health Inequality Unit, 2007) as w ell as having  a shorter  life oneself. The same is true for infant mortality. The list of measurements of poorer health in low social classes not  assessed in this essay is long. Such    are inequalities in   lung can cer rates , cardiovascular diseases , accidents and suicides, respiratory diseases or obesity (Department of Health, 2009). All of those health factors led to worse outcomes the lower the social class. As a result, those in a lower  class have to deal with an enormous      numbers of negative  consequences, or  put simple, ba d health o f t hemselves and relativ es. The out come in terms  of heal th t herefore builds the first reason to seen inequalities as problematic.However, the consequences relieve only half of  the injustice. In  lower social cla sses there is a  higher p revalence of social an d psychological factors such as stress, anxieties or depression. So the lives in the lower classes are on  the one h and s horter due  to worse m edical conditions. And  on the o ther  hand they are less joyful, more fill ed with s tress factors. Wilkinson calls this a  ´bubble inequality´ and ´life is short where its quality is poor´ (Wilkinson, 2005).

In addition to the outcomes of p oor health  the major reason why ine qualities are s een as a problem st ems from   the  development  of s ocial class es. For  child ren, s ocial  class is determined by the  parents and cha nging th e social  class throug hout one's own lifetime i  s difficult to  achieve and in many   cases it  is  not  possible (Health Inequality Unit,   2007). Inequalities start before birth (smoking during pregnancy, children vaccine), at an age where the indivi dual does n ot have an y influen ce at  his or her own lifestyl e. Although r andomly being bor n into one or  the other social cl ass does not displ ay any injus tice per se. But the fact that f rom the early beginn ing life is d etermined by a s ocial construct, a social  injustice where th e i ndividual does not ha  ve an y influ ence on, is unfair . An d th erefore it is als o problematic.

Generally inequalities in health due to social class are both socially *unfair* and *problematic*. Health inequalities effect major parts of the population (remember, 28% of the population is in the Sp earhead Group). Th e wel l-being o f t he en tire p opulation can ther efore only b e improved through *major social changes.* That way, it can be achieved what the World Health Organization, calls "Health": A "state of complete physical, mental, and social well-being and not merely the absence of disease or infirmity".

## Table of Figures

# Bibliography

Black, D., Morris, J., Smith, C. and Townsend, P. (1980) *Inequalities in Health: Report of a Working Party*, London: Department of Health and Social Security.

Department of Health (2008) *Tackling H ealth Inequaliti es: 2007 S tatus Repor t on the Program for Action*, Report, London: Department of Health

Department of H ealth (2009) *Tackling Heal th Inequaliti es: 10 Years On – A review of developments in tackling health inequalit ies in England over the last 10 years*, Repor t, London: Department of Health

Health Inequality Uni t, Department of Health (2007) *Tackling Health In equalities: 2004-06 data and policy update for the 2010 National Target*, Report, London: Department of Health

Macintyre, S. (2002) ` Before and After the Black Report: Four Fallacies`, in Berridge, V. and Blume, S. (eds) *Poor Health: Social Inequalities before and after th e Black Report*, London: Frank Cass, pp 198-219

National Health Ser vice (2004) *Choosing h ealth: Making health choices easier*, C m 6374, London: Stationery Office

Office of National Statistics (2010) ` *NS-SEC classes and collapses* `. Available at http://www.ons.gov.uk/about-statistics/classifications/current/ns-sec/cats-and-classes/ns-sec-classes-and-collapses/index.html[Accessed 8th December 2010]

Wilkinson, R. G. (1996) *Unhealthy Societies: The Afflictions of Inequality*, London: Routledge

Wilkinson, R. G. (2005) *The Imp act of Inequalities: How t o make sick societies healthier*, London, Routledge